About the Author

Elizabeth Minikel is passionate about evangelism and joyfully shares about Jesus with anyone who is willing to listen. She has done mission work for various organizations in the United States and internationally. She has had a front-row seat to see how God's love changes hearts and transforms lives. She has a heart for evangelism; and enjoys teaching and training others to be bold and courageous in sharing their faith. Elizabeth lives with her husband, Bryan, in North Carolina. They enjoy spending time outdoors, traveling, and being the proud aunt and uncle to their amazing nieces and nephews.

Burdened Hearts
By Jesus' Wounds, You Are Healed

Elizabeth Minikel

Burdened Hearts
By Jesus' Wounds, You Are Healed

Olympia Publishers
London

www.olympiapublishers.com
OLYMPIA PAPERBACK EDITION

Copyright © Elizabeth Minikel 2024

The right of Elizabeth Minikel to be identified as the author of this work has been asserted in accordance with sections 77 and 78 of the Copyright, Designs and Patents Act 1988.

All Rights Reserved

No reproduction, copy or transmission of this publication may be made without written permission.
No paragraph of this publication may be reproduced, copied or transmitted save with the written permission of the publisher, or in accordance with the provisions of the Copyright Act 1956 (as amended).

Any person who commits any unauthorized act in relation to this publication may be liable to criminal prosecution and civil claims for damage.

A CIP catalogue record for this title is available from the British Library.

ISBN: 978-1-80439-824-1

As with all times of sorrow, if you or someone you know is struggling beyond what they can handle, always seek professional medical care. Never hesitate to get the professional attention you need either for yourself or for someone else.

First Published in 2024

Olympia Publishers
Tallis House
2 Tallis Street
London
EC4Y 0AB

Printed in Great Britain

Copyright

Scripture quotations marked CSB have been taken from the Christian Standard Bible®, Copyright © 2017 by Holman Bible Publishers. Used by permission. Christian Standard Bible® and CSB® are federally registered trademarks of Holman Bible Publishers.

Scripture quotations marked (NASB) are taken from the (NASB®) New American Standard Bible ®, Copyright © 1960, 1971, 1977, 1995, 2020 by The Lockman Foundation. Used by permission. All rights reserved. lockman.org

Scripture quotations marked (NIV) are taken from the Holy Bible , New International Version®, NIV®. Copyright © 1973, 1978, 1984, 2011 by Biblica, Inc.™ Used by permission of Zondervan. All rights reserved worldwide. www.zondervan.comThe "NIV" and "New International Version" are trademarks registered in the United States Patent and Trademark Office by Biblica, Inc.™

Scripture quotations marked (NLT) are taken from the Holy Bible, New Living Translation, copyright ©1996, 2004, 2015 by Tyndale House Foundation. Used by permission of Tyndale House Publishers, Carol Stream, Illinois 60188. All rights reserved.

Scripture quotations marked (NKJV) are taken from the New King James Version®. Copyright © 1982 by Thomas Nelson. Used by permission. All rights reserved.

Dedication

Ruth, this book is dedicated to you in memory of Fred Minikel. It was your love for your husband and your words of encouragement that inspired me to write this book.

Acknowledgements

In my life, the greatest gifts God has given me have come in the precious form of people. I would like to say an enormous thank-you to some of those wonderful God-given gifts. Kara Smith, my heart overflows with gratitude at the countless hours you poured into the original manuscript. Your mastery of the English language and ability to see the beauty in everything transformed every word to read a million times better. Rachel Law, your love for Christ and others, shines bright in everything you do. Thank you for all the help, wisdom, and expertise you put into the book and that you gave to me personally. To the incredible, Rita Walker and Margo Madsen, I cannot thank you both enough for being willing to meticulously comb through every letter, word, and exclamation point. You both are amazingly talented at what you do, and I am so grateful for your servant's hearts. Sara Christiansen, thank you for your continuous prayers, support, and encouragement. A special thanks to Pastor John Reece, for verifying that the Scripture references were biblically accurate and relevant. I will never be able to thank you enough for how you have spiritually poured into and encouraged my walk with the Lord throughout the years. To my sister, Melissa Pancoast, thank you for brainstorming thoughts and ideas with me. I am overflowing with gratitude to God for giving us both the gift of shared missionary experiences, where we have the joy of sharing the love of Jesus everywhere we go. Finally, to the love of my life,

Bryan Minikel. No words would ever be enough to express the joy you have given me in our lives together. Thank you for your faithfulness, your support, and this beautiful life we share together. May our love for each other be our most precious testimony of His love for us. To God be all the Glory.

Preface

My desire in writing this devotional is that you will meet Jesus in the following pages. That the story of His love for you will begin to mend the sorrow in your heart, as you discover who Jesus is and what He did for you. This book of encouragement is for anyone with a burdened heart; whether you have walked with the Lord for years, days, or have never heard the name of Jesus.

Over these next forty days, my hope is that you will be joyfully inspired, to continue to put one foot in front of the other as we move through this journey together. Hand in hand we will discover the peace and joy of Christ, no matter what circumstances or challenges we face. These devotions were initially inspired by letters of encouragement, comfort, and strength to a beloved friend after losing her loved one. Only when I took pen in hand, did something transformative happen inside my heart. I discovered that when I opened my Bible and poured over who God is and the love He has for us, I began writing to my friend, and myself. My heart became filled with hope, as I meditated on the promises of God. Within those pages, I rediscovered His faithfulness, goodness, and sovereignty in a new and beautiful way. My heart became overjoyed and uplifted as my eyes were opened to the peace and strength He gives us as we seek Him during the most difficult and trying times in our lives.

In those times, those very difficult circumstances, don't gloss over the presence of His goodness and faithfulness that surround you. His mercies and comfort will give you strength in your time of need. I hope your heart, ears, and eyes will be open to perceive how the world's brokenness and heartache scream out about the existence of God. That pain you feel points to the centrality of the gospel message; God didn't leave us to suffer alone. No! Instead, Jesus stepped into our suffering, and died for our sins, so that through faith in Him we have the promise of eternal life (John 3:16). The gospel reveals that the God of the universe meets us in our brokenness and tells us we are loved and that He wants to know us personally. How beautiful the Good News is for the hurting soul.

Friend, I pray that over this forty-day journey, your heart and mind will begin to see Jesus in a brand-new way. That you will see Him with new eyes as your Friend (John 15:15), Comforter (2 Corinthians 1:3-4), and Good Shepherd (John 10:11). Know that you are perfectly loved by Him and that He sees you in your sorrow. Therefore, be prepared to hear the sweet sound of the words, "God loves you", over and over again. His compassionate grace and mercy for you is indescribable within the limits of language, and it is a gift that's receivable by you. A love that He richly lavishes down on us from heaven, even when we don't deserve or ask for it. Friend, you are loved!

Finally, I would encourage you to read these devotionals and spend time in His Word (The Bible) and prayer. Each devotional includes multiple Bible translations of scripture verses. The reason for my choice in these translations is simply that these are the translations I prefer reading, studying, and reflecting on in my own daily study. As you read, you will discover some Bible references do not include a specific translation. For these instances, choose a translation that works best for you. At the end of each of the forty days, I have included a short prayer as an inspirational example for your daily prayer time with God. As with all times of sorrow, if you or someone you know is struggling beyond what they can handle, always seek professional medical care. Never hesitate to get the professional attention you need either for yourself or for someone else. I hope my words bring you strength and comfort as God begins to mend your heart with the peace and joy found in Him.

> To the *hurting*, Jesus offers comfort.
> To the *searching*, Jesus offers wisdom and truth.
> To the *insecure*, Jesus offers self-worth.
> To the *weary*, Jesus offers rest.
> To the *broken-hearted,* Jesus mends hearts.
> To the *lost*, Jesus offers life.
> To the *disheartened*, Jesus offers hope.
> To the *forgotten*, Jesus calls them by name.
> To the *burdened*, Jesus takes the load.
> To the *sick*, Jesus offers healing.
> To the *fearful*, Jesus offers peace.
> To the *unloved* and *rejected*, Jesus offers unconditional love.
> To the *discontent*, Jesus offers satisfaction.
> To those who are wanting *meaning* and *dignity*,
> Jesus gives each and every person value, meaning, and purpose.
> To those *seeking* a way to God, Jesus offers the way.

Day 1: Trouble

Friend, you are not alone in your heartache. You are not alone in your brokenness and sorrow. In this world, if trouble is not knocking at our door, it may be perched just outside the window. Jesus promised that in this world we will have troubles. Each and every one of us. No one is exempt from trouble. The question is not *if* difficulties will come your way, but *what will you do* when they arrive?

Jesus said, "I have told you these things, so that in me you may have peace. In this world you will have trouble. But take heart! I have overcome the world" (John 16:33 NIV).

We may be surrounded by trouble on all sides, but Jesus promises that in Him we will find the peace that our souls have been desperately seeking. Jesus is our refuge when the troubles of the world feel as though they are closing in around us. Jesus gives us peace that is not of this world, so we never have to be afraid of the circumstances we face. Jesus said, "Peace I leave with you; my peace I give you. I do not give to you as the world gives. Do not let your hearts be troubled and do not be afraid" (John 14:27 NIV).

You are unconditionally loved by the One who created you. A Heavenly Father who graciously meets us in the middle of our sorrows will give us the strength, comfort, and peace that we yearn for in our darkest hour. We can rest assured knowing that He is always faithful and He is always good. Your sorrows, your pain, and your troubles are not wasted in Him. *In this life, you may not know why you endured your battles, but you can joyfully trust that God will work out everything for the good of His children and ultimately for His glory.*

"And we know that God causes everything to work together for the good of those who love God and are called according to his purpose for them. For God knew his people in advance, and he chose them to become like his Son, so that his Son would be the firstborn among many brothers and sisters" (Romans 8:28-29 NLT).

As children of God, we trust that our Heavenly Father is working out everything for our good even when the circumstances in our life might not necessarily be good in themselves. God's Word reveals to us that brokenness exists in this fallen world because of sin. It is in God's plan of redemption that everything can be used for His glory as He works out all things for your good out of His great love for you. It is during this time that we, as followers of Christ, are being made more like Christ—which is our ultimate pursuit and desire! We joyfully wait on the Lord, trusting His faithfulness and goodness in the middle of whatever situation we face. Our seasons of suffering may wash over us like tidal waves, but the water eventually recedes and returns to the sea. We must ask ourselves, "Am I trusting God's goodness and faithfulness in the middle of my suffering? Am I praising God *even though* I am facing hardship and trials?"

What if one of the greatest gifts you receive in this life, is wrapped in your deepest sorrow? Today is the day to see your troubles with a new perspective; as our hearts and eyes are focused on Jesus. Trusting that no matter what troubles we face, God is with us, loving us, and using our situation to make us more like Christ! We delight that God is working in the midst of our sorrow, for the good of His children! Friend, know this: God knows every sorrow, every tear, and every single trouble you have faced. God knows it all. He knows every single tear you have cried. God knows, and He cares. Friend, He knows your sorrow and sees your trouble and He loves you more than you could ever hope or imagine! You are not alone. "You keep track of all my sorrows. You have collected all my tears in your bottle. You have recorded each one in your book" (Psalm 56:8 NLT).

Prayer

Heavenly Father,
You see my every tear. You know my every sorrow. You know every trouble I face, even before I face it. Thank You that no matter what circumstance I am going through, You are with me. You give me everything I need. I rejoice that in this life You give me Your peace. I am not afraid, nor is my heart troubled, because of Your goodness, faithfulness, and love. I joyfully enter into prayer with an expectant heart, eager to come alongside You in the work You are already doing in my life because You love me. I thank and praise You for today, tomorrow, and whatever is to come, for You are good and You are good to me. In Jesus' name, amen.

"You will keep in perfect peace those whose minds are steadfast, because they trust in you" (Isaiah 26:3 NIV).

Day 2: Life-Transforming Love

"Your love, LORD, reaches to the heavens, your faithfulness to the skies. Your righteousness is like the highest mountains, your justice like the great deep. You, LORD, preserve both people and animals. How priceless is your unfailing love, O God! People take refuge in the shadow of your wings. They feast on the abundance of your house; you give them drink from your river of delights. For with you is the fountain of life; in your light we see light" (Psalm 36:5-9 NIV).

How great is God's love for you! The love of our God is unconditional. His love is not dependent on anything you could ever say or do. His steadfast love for you is irrevocable, it is pure, unchanging and it is not contingent. *God's love for us is unfailing. Our human love is only a speck in the vastness of the galaxy in comparison to the love the Creator of the universe has for you.* The One who knows you, who formed you, and who lovingly knit you in your mother's womb (Psalm 139:14-15 NIV) is the same God who created all things (Genesis 1:1). He is the God who gave you breath in your lungs, the heart in your chest, and all the wonderfully unique characteristics that make you who you are. Your life has purpose and meaning, you are not an accident, mistake, or mishap. God's unfailing love for us is deeper than our understanding. God's love is more wonderful than our hearts could ever hope for and His love for us is greater than our minds could possibly imagine. God's love for us trumps all other loves by comparison. Friend, God's love for you is real and His love is tangible. God loves you! God loves you! God loves you!

God sees you right now. He knows what you have endured and are currently enduring. Nothing escapes Him, absolutely nothing. The love God has for us is not equivalent to the love of anything we have ever experienced or will experience in our lives. His love is perfect. No matter what sorrow, loss, or heartache you have felt, there is a Father in heaven who cares about you. As a believer in Christ, you are chosen and adopted by God (Ephesians 1:4-6). The same hands that formed the universe belong to the One who knows us better than we know ourselves. He will never let His sons and daughters go. As believers, we look forward to the promise of eternal life in heaven with Jesus. The joy we have in Christ starts right here, right now, on earth, the moment we put our faith in Jesus. For we know that no matter what hardship or circumstances we face, we are in our Father's hands (John 10:29). We rejoice because we are deeply loved and we are cared for every single day of our lives. *God is the Potter and His people are the clay (Isaiah 64:8), as He carefully shapes and molds us into a glorious likeness of His Son.*

"But now, LORD, You are our Father; We are the clay, and You our potter, And all of us are the work of Your hand" (Isaiah 64:8 NASB).

The process of this shaping can be slow and difficult at times. As His child, learn to trust His faithful and compassionate work in you. As His creation, we know that you are lovingly and joyfully cradled in His hands. Our beautiful new frames, which were once fragmented and fractured by life's circumstances, shine brightly with Christ. God's work in us has made us ready and capable of enduring life's troubles. We are the work of His hands for His glory!

Prayer

Heavenly Father,
Thank You for the indescribable gift of Your love, which is like a salve to my hurting heart. Love is not just something You do; love is Who You are. Your love continually transforms me, making me more like Your Son, Jesus Christ. I can see and feel the fingerprints of Your love imprinted across my heart and across my life; for You have always been with me, from beginning to end. Thank You that through faith in Christ, we are adopted into Your family; as Your sons and Your daughters. Your Word says, "But to all who did receive him, he gave them the right to be children of God, to those who believe in his name" (John 1:12 CSB). In Jesus' name, amen.

"For he chose us in him, before the foundation of the world, to be holy and blameless in love before him. He predestined us to be adopted as sons through Jesus Christ for himself, according to the good pleasure of his will, to the praise of his glorious grace that he has lavished on us in the Beloved One" (Ephesians 1:4-6 CSB).

Day 3: New Mercies, New Day, New Beginnings!

"Yet I call this to mind, and therefore I have hope: Because of the LORD's faithful love we do not perish, for his mercies never end. They are new every morning; great is your faithfulness! I say, 'The LORD is my portion therefore I will put my hope in him" (Lamentations 3:21-24 CSB).

Our troubles may surround us like the darkness of night, but God's mercies are made new for you every morning. As the morning light shines down on you, feel God's love, comfort, and mercy pour over you and into your life. As the light emerges over the horizon, we are reminded that no matter what suffering we are enduring, we have reason for hope. God is faithful, and He is good. His love never fails! No matter what circumstance we face, as believers we have already been given the most amazing gift; the gift of God with us. God promises to be with us always; regardless of the obstacles or hardships that come our way. The Lord is our portion, our happiness, our joy, and our soul's delight. In Him, we find everything we need. As you open your eyes today, remember; that God's mercies are new for you today. "This is the day the LORD has made; let's rejoice and be glad in it" (Psalm 118:24 CSB).

Daily, uncountable blessings and miracles from God rain down all around us, beautiful little gifts from heaven above. *Have you been keeping your eyes open to God's gifts from heaven so that you can unwrap, thank, and cherish them all?* These everyday gifts consist from heaven consist of breath in our lungs, a favorite meal we enjoy, or time spent with a loved one or pet. At other times, His miracles manifest themselves in our protection on the roadways, the durability and sustainability of everyday things we depend on, like our cars and appliances, or when He protects and keeps our bodies healthy. We are surrounded by God's mercies every single day. God is working in ways we cannot even imagine that are for our good and for His glory, His honor, and for His name. Thank God for the miracles upon miracles He pours out on us daily. Lord, open our eyes to see them and have a joyful heart of thankfulness and gladness! "A joyful heart is good medicine, but a broken spirit dries up the bones" (Proverbs 17:22 CSB).

All the things that fill your heart with emptiness—your discouragement, shame, discontentment, and regret; give it to God as you turn to Him in prayer and time in His Word. Satan knows your past, but he does not have the capability to know what is in your future. Only God does! You have the ability to choose to lay down the things that darken your attitude and choose to do the things that bring joy and hope to your life. Even if the obstacles you are facing today feel daunting, remember that God is with you. Ask Him daily to help you exchange your attitude and perspective for His strength and His comfort. This very minute is your turning point to change your outlook; as you seek Him first and empty your burdens into His hands.

Today is the day to start living a new chapter with a heart of radical gratefulness and unshakeable hope. As you daily spend time abiding in the presence of your Heavenly Father, gladly take a seat at the table where God is already providing you with all you need. As He fills your plate full of His peace and His joy, remember that is a peace that is not of this world, as it never runs out. Your cup overflows and your heart becomes thankful because you are reminded just how much God loves and cares for you.

Prayer

Heavenly Father,

I welcome Your mercies with arms wide open, as today is a gift from You. Transform my burdened heart into a cheerful heart, because it finds its joy in You, and not in my circumstances. As I open my eyes to a brand-new day, I am reminded of the prison of brokenness and discouragement I have locked myself in. Help me to live today with my eyes on Jesus, and not continuing to stare at my own heartache in the rearview mirror. Take away my past faults, failures, and imperfections that I have allowed defining who I am. When my heart becomes downcast and discouraged, remind me of Your continued faithfulness and promises. Restore, renew, and refresh my thoughts and attitude in a way that brings You glory. I thank and praise You for Your Word says, "Now all glory to God, who is able, through his mighty power at work within us, to accomplish infinitely more than we might ask or think" (Ephesians 3:20 NLT). In Jesus' name, amen.

"Now may the God of hope fill you with all joy and peace in believing, so that you will abound in hope by the power of the Holy Spirit" (Romans 15:13 NASB).

Day 4: Fearfully and Wonderfully Knit Together

"For you created my inmost being; you knit me together in my mother's womb. I praise you because I am fearfully and wonderfully made; your works are wonderful, I know that full well. My frame was not hidden from you when I was made in the secret place, when I was woven together in the depths of the earth. Your eyes saw my unformed body; all the days ordained for me were written in your book before one of them came to be. How precious to me are your thoughts, God! How vast is the sum of them! Were I to count them, they would outnumber the grains of sand—when I awake, I am still with you" (Psalm 139:13-18 NIV).

Hear these wonderful words of life: *You were created by God. Friend, you were made in His image.* "So God created man in His *own* image; in the image of God He created him; male and female He created them" (Genesis 1:27 NKJV).

You have dignity, worth, and significance. Your life has value. Friend, if you have air in your lungs and blood in your body, God has a purpose and a plan for your life. He has it all planned out. You are not a mistake, you are not defined by your past, and you cannot add even a minute to your life. What joy this gives us, knowing that all our days are accounted for by our Heavenly Father, who loves and cares for us. Fill your hearts and lives with the hope and assurance that all of our days are intended by God?

Jesus is calling you *today* to live a life that is full of purpose and meaning. To live a life glorifying God with everything you are; joyfully trusting Him to provide everything we need. As our broken hearts begin to heal, we begin a new adventure of living in the love of Christ. To begin living in a way that impacts the world around us, pointing them to Jesus. Jesus calls us to come as we are, giving Him the pieces of our brokenness, for in Him we are made whole. When we become discouraged by the circumstances and trials we face, we keep our eyes on Jesus. Knowing that in Him we have the fullness of life. As believers, we have an abundant life in Christ no matter what we face. "The thief comes only to steal and kill and destroy; I have come that they may have life and have it to the full" (John 10:10 NIV).

What this means is that we don't have to remain in our brokenness. We can be wholly healed and made new in Christ. You are loved. You have worth and value and your life has meaning. God has a purpose for you and a plan for your life. The Israelites constantly walked away from God, yet He always remained steadfast and faithful to them. He never left them, nor abandoned them. Read the words God spoke to the Israelites while they were in exile: "For I know the plans I have for you,' declares the LORD, 'plans for prosperity and not for disaster, to give you a future and a hope. Then you will call upon Me and come and pray to Me, and I will listen to you. And you will seek Me and find *Me* when you search for Me with all your heart" (Jeremiah 29:11-13 NASB).

First and foremost, our identity, as Christians, is in Christ. We don't have to worry about *who* we are, as our identity is firmly built on the One who made us. We are not our highest highs or our lowest lows. Friend, we are not defined by our failures nor by our successes. We are His. As children of God, we are loved and chosen even before we are born. God loved us from the very beginning. It is because of who we are in Christ, that we don't have to second guess anything. We go forward in full assurance that we are loved and find our satisfaction in God. The gospel is not just a future hope, it is hope we have today, right now, in Christ!

Prayer

Heavenly Father,
I thank You and praise You for the life you have given me. I thank You that You always see me, wherever I am. My life has meaning because of You. I never have to worry if I have value or meaning because I am who You say I am. Thank You that through faith in Christ Jesus, I have a hope that lasts forever. I am free to live every day in You because You already know all my days, nothing is out of Your sovereign control. In Jesus' name, amen.

> "Know that the LORD, He *is* God; *It is* He *who* has made us, and not we ourselves;
> *We are* His people and the sheep of His pasture"
> (Psalm 100:3 NKJV).

Day 5: No More Worries, Only Worship

"Rejoice in the Lord always. I will say it again: Rejoice! Let your graciousness be known to everyone. The Lord is near. Don't worry about anything, but in everything, through prayer and petition with thanksgiving, present your requests to God. And the peace of God, which surpasses all understanding, will guard your hearts and minds in Christ Jesus. Finally, brothers and sisters, whatever is true, whatever is honorable, whatever is just, whatever is pure, whatever is lovely, whatever is commendable—if there is any moral excellence and if there is anything praiseworthy—dwell on these things" (Philippians 4:4-8 CSB).

God invites us to turn our worries into praise! We don't have to worry about today or tomorrow because God holds it all in His sovereign hands. Trusting Him to take care of every need can help us substitute our anxiety for worship. We give Him every situation and every hardship we face, and we thank Him that He's already got it. How often do our own worries leave us stranded and unable to go forward in faith and in confidence! As believers, we do not have joy because of the outward circumstances we face, we have joy because it originates from the hope we have in Christ. He is our ultimate joy, and we always have this joy, despite any hardships and worries that come our way!

As sons and daughters of God, the peace we experience comes from knowing that God is in control of all things. Friend, when you truly trust God with your worries, what kind of beautiful peace would that bring you? What kind of wonderful, life-transforming joy would transcend your heart and mind? Allow these life-giving words to soak into your heart so that you are ready when the wheels of worry start to turn. As believers, we hide God's Word in our hearts so that we know His Truth and know who we are in Christ.

When we have the Word of God in our hearts, we will not be overcome with worry or fear. When we have meditated on His truths and promises, our hearts will become firmly planted in our hope in Christ. Our identity in Christ defeats and tears down every worry, self-loathing thought, and accusatory statement. In Christ, there is no condemnation (Romans 8:1). Who could easily defeat a man and woman of God who has prepared their hearts and minds in defense of Satan's antics? Today is the day to start a new life and a brand-new beginning in Christ. When you are born-again as a Christian, you are a new creation. "Therefore, if anyone is in Christ, *this person is* a new creation; the old things passed away; behold, new things have come" (2 Corinthians 5:17 NASB).

We already know who we are. We are children of our Heavenly Father. As children of God, our identity is in Jesus. We are not to be controlled by our thoughts and fears. We have the power of God in us, and with Christ we can overcome. We take every fear and lie of Satan and turn it around into worship. We give God every thought that says we aren't *"good enough"*. We give Him every thought that says we are a *"failure"*. We give Him every thought that says *"Our circumstances will never change"*. We turn those thoughts into worship, praise, and thanksgiving. *As a child of God, you are redeemed, and you are loved*! We are made new from the inside out, and we worship God with our lives. Worship is not something contained within the four walls of a building, worship is what we do every day. We worship God with how we live our lives, in our actions, and with the words we say each day.

Prayer

Heavenly Father,
You know how often my heart is divided between You and the cares of the world. How often do I become so laser- focused on life's distractions, that I miss You? I grow accustomed to the bombardment of my worries that I forget Your perfect peace. Renew and transform my mind, replacing my pitfalls with Your Word. Inspire my heart to turn to You, not just in the turbulent times, but in every moment of the day. Turn the worry that dominates my inner being into audacious worship and praise. May the everlasting hope I have in Christ well up in my heart and seep inside every sinew and fiber of my being, so that my fears have no room to stay. As I reflect on Your innumerable blessings, You pour out on us from above. I am completely overwhelmed by Your love. Remind me that when the troubles and hardships of the day are many, Your mercies are more! How beautiful is Your grace! May I never grow tired of recounting the wonderment of the cross. In Jesus' name, amen.

"Therefore, brothers and sisters, in view of the mercies of God, I urge you to present your bodies as a living sacrifice, holy and pleasing to God; this is your true worship. Do not be conformed to this age, but be transformed by the renewing of your mind, so that you may discern what is the good, pleasing, and perfect will of God" (Romans 12:1-2 CSB).

Day 6: He Is Our Comforter

"Praise be to the God and Father of our Lord Jesus Christ, the Father of compassion and the God of all comfort, who comforts us in all our troubles so that we can comfort those in any trouble with the comfort we ourselves receive from God. For just as we share abundantly in the sufferings of Christ, so also our comfort abounds through Christ. If we are distressed, it is for your comfort and salvation; if we are comforted, it is for your comfort, which produces in you patient endurance of the same sufferings we suffer. And our hope for you is firm because we know that just as you share in our sufferings, so also you share in our comfort" (2 Corinthians 1:3-7 NIV).

You have a story! Yes, you! You have a story of how God has worked in your life. A story of how He has continued to show you His unfailing love and provided all that you needed as you faced life's circumstances. *Consider this, had you not gone through your hardship, would you be the same person you are today?*

Suffering does two things: it *puts a microscope on our lives, revealing our hearts, while simultaneously positioning a magnifying glass on Who God is and His love for us.* This microscope can either reveal our lives becoming more like Christ as we produce more character, hope, and perseverance; or it can zoom in on our bitterness and hardness of heart. Meanwhile, this magnifying glass also amplifies God's faithfulness, goodness, mercy, and love. A beautiful and powerful display of His love. *We are gifted with the ability to see a whole new side of God we would have never seen; had we not experienced our circumstances.* We see a God who comforts us as He lovingly gives us the encouragement, confidence, strength, and hope that we need.

Placing a microscope on our brokenness can make us feel exposed and laid bare, but the beauty of this transparency is that others catch a glimpse of who we truly are; not the made-up version we sometimes like to portray. They see the *real* us, and a very real God who is doing real work in our lives. God can take our greatest falls and failures and turn them into good. God can transform what Satan, our enemy, intended for our destruction to become a bright beacon pointing others to the hope we have found in Christ. God can use your story of brokenness to speak into the hearts and lives of others who face similar trials. What if the pain you endured changed the life of even one person that they might know Christ? *Would this life's temporary heartache be worth one person's eternal soul?* What a beautiful story of redemption each and every one of His children has to share with the whole world.

That's the beauty of God's kingdom, which is wonderfully different from the world around us. We are called to love others even though we may be broken ourselves. We can connect with others because the perfect love of God has radically transformed our hearts so that we are free to joyfully love people without expecting anything in return. *Friend, be the love of Christ to someone today as you comfort them in their brokenness and sorrow.* What joy and healing it will produce in your heart as you pour into someone else today. If you feel unqualified or uncomfortable sharing, then you are in the right place! Turn your burdened heart toward the things our Heavenly Father cares about and He will place a passion on your heart for the lost, the oppressed, the widow, and the orphan (Isaiah 1:17 NIV). If you have a heart for injustice, that was put there by God. God placed you wherever you are so that you would be a witness, pointing others to the One who meets people in their brokenness. Who reached out His hands to heal those who were considered untouchable (Matthew 8:3). We reach out to others so that they also would know the One who loves and cares for them.

Today is the day to embrace the excitement of the Samaritan woman at the well who ran to tell the whole town about the One she has just met (John 4:28-29). Today is the day to rejoice in the heart transformation of Paul who was radically changed by his encounter with Jesus on the road to Damascus (Acts 9:3-6).

Prayer

Heavenly Father,
May the beauty of the gospel be fresh in my heart every morning, leaving a new zest and zeal for everything I do. Open my ears to be a good listener to whomever You place in my path today; with a heart sympathetic and compassionate, like You! Help me to intentionally share Your love and be a comfort to others in the way You were a comfort to me. As Your Word says, "Let, I pray, Your merciful kindness be for my comfort, According to Your word to Your servant" (Psalm 119:76 NKJV). In the beautiful name of Jesus, amen.

"Blessed *are* the poor in spirit, For theirs is the kingdom of heaven. Blessed *are* those that mourn, For they shall be comforted" (Matthew 5:3-4 NKJV).

Day 7: Whatever the Circumstances

"For I am persuaded that neither death nor life, nor angels nor principalities nor powers, nor things present nor things to come, nor height nor depth, nor any other created thing, shall be able to separate us from the love of God which is in Christ Jesus our Lord" (Romans 8:38-39 NKJV).

Paul learned how to be content in all situations because he knew one of the most beautiful truths of the Christian faith: *Our Christian joy is not found in this world but in Jesus Himself.* When we make God the ultimate treasure and delight of our hearts, it doesn't matter what circumstances we face, because we don't derive our ultimate gratification from any created things; like our jobs, relationships, hobbies, or families. Created things always have the potential to let us down, but the Creator Himself never will. Where you lack happiness, He will supply you with His peace and His joy. Where you lack the ability to love and forgive, simply look to Christ for the perfect example. His power is sufficient in our suffering and He knows just what we need at just the right time.

Paul knew suffering and He knew it well! Our hearts gasp at the extreme suffering and hardships Paul faced, for the advancement of the gospel. God's plan for Paul's life was full of pain and constant troubles: "Five times I received the forty lashes minus one from the Jews. Three times I was beaten with rods.

Once I received a stoning. Three times I was shipwrecked. I have spent a night and a day in the open sea. On frequent journeys, I faced dangers from rivers, dangers from robbers, dangers from my own people, dangers from Gentiles, dangers in the city, dangers in the wilderness, dangers at sea, and dangers among false brothers; toil and hardship, many sleepless nights, hunger and thirst, often without food, cold, and without clothing" (2 Corinthians 11:24-27 CSB).

As a former zealous persecutor of the early church, his life was forever changed when he encountered Jesus on the road to Damascus. Paul was being called by God to proclaim the gospel (Acts 9:13-15). Even with the hard circumstances he faced, Paul wrote, "I don't say this out of need, for I have learned to be content in whatever circumstances I find myself. I know how to make do with little, and I know how to make do with a lot. In any and all circumstances I have learned the secret of being content—whether well fed or hungry, whether in abundance or in need. I am able to do all things through him who strengthens me" (Philippians 4:11-13 CSB). He was able to say these words because he knew where to find his strength. His strength was in the Lord! *We never have to question God's sovereignty or His omnipotence.* Because God is all powerful (Psalm 147:5), knowing all things (1 John 3:20), and always for our good (Romans 8:28).

We don't have to remain guilty for our past mistakes or disheartened by our current circumstances. *We just simply need to trust Him.* Trust that He will always give us what we need to face and endure whatever circumstances come our way. God doesn't need *our* strength; for His power is limitless. He doesn't need our money, for He is the Creator of everything. What God desires is our hearts! So, keep your eyes on Jesus, friend. Whatever hardships or trials you may encounter are not worth comparing to the joy you have in Christ. Child of God lay down your disappointments and failures and look forward to the crown of life Christ promises to those who love Him. Be encouraged by the hope you have today in Christ Jesus.

Prayer

Heavenly Father,
I delight in Your Word that says, "The hidden things belong to the LORD our God, but the revealed things belong to us and to our children forever, so that we may follow all the words of this law" (Deuteronomy 29:29 CSB). My heart rejoices that You know all things. You see my story from beginning to end, and I trust Your goodness and sovereignty to use my story for Your ultimate goal. I rest in the fact that everything is in Your hands and in Your control. There is not one random particle or tiny speck that hides from Your sight. Give me Your strength to endure; to overcome whatever circumstances I face. May You receive the glory! In Jesus' name, amen.

"Blessed is the one who endures trials, because when he has stood the test he will receive the crown of life that God has promised to those who love him" (James 1:12 CSB).

Day 8: The Radicalness of Grace

"And be kind to one another, tenderhearted, forgiving one another, even as God in Christ forgave you" (Ephesians 4:32 NKJV).

She was known. Known for her immorality. As she entered the house of Simon the Pharisee, she knew Jesus would be there, as He had been invited to dinner. She took her beautiful alabaster jar of expensive perfume and knelt behind Jesus, at His feet crying. The tears that fell onto His feet with her hair as she kissed His feet, wiped with her hair. She kisses His feet, putting her expensive perfume over them (Luke 7:36-38 NLT).

"When the Pharisee who had invited him saw this, he said to himself, 'If this man were a prophet, he would know what kind of woman is touching him. She's a sinner!"

"Then Jesus answered his thoughts. 'Simon,' he said to the Pharisee, 'I have something to say to you."

"Go ahead, Teacher,' Simon replied."

"Then Jesus told him this story: 'A man loaned money to two people—500 pieces of silver to one and 50 pieces to the other. But neither of them could repay him, so he kindly forgave them both, canceling their debts. Who do you suppose loved him more after that?"

"Simon answered, 'I suppose the one for whom he canceled the larger debt."

"That's right,' Jesus said. Then he turned to the woman and said to Simon, 'Look at this woman kneeling here. When I entered your home, you didn't offer me any water to wash the dust off my feet, but she has washed them with her tears and wiped them with her hair. You didn't greet me with a kiss, but from the time I first came in, she has not stopped kissing my feet. You neglected the courtesy of olive oil to anoint my head, but she has anointed my feet with rare perfume. I tell you, her sins— and they are many—have been forgiven, so she has shown me much love. But a person who is forgiven little shows only little love" (Luke 7:39-47 NLT).

Forgiving another for the pain they have caused; without harboring any resentment does not easily come to our human nature. Our hearts are quick to clamp down on the searing words and hurtful actions that cut us so deep; allowing our agony to fuel our sorrow. Our stubborn refusal to forgive relinquishes our freedom to live joyfully and keeps us in a bondage of bitterness. We grow weary under the burden we are unable to carry, a burden we weren't meant to carry. But in Christ, it is within the ashes of brokenness, that the remarkable beauty of the gospel shines bright. Jesus, who never sinned (2 Corinthians 5:21), died for you and me so that our debt against God would be paid in full (Colossians 2:13-14).

When we compare our earthly grievances to those we have

committed against a perfect God, our heart's perspective shifts in view of the cross. *To forgive is a gift from God, liberating our own hearts from bitterness and anger.* The woman with the alabaster jar wholly understood the life altering grace we find in Christ, and because of that understanding, she passionately worshiped Jesus. *When we grasp the grace God so loving offers us, how can we do anything else but fall at His feet and worship?* We cannot help but be transformed by His grace. It is because of our changed hearts that we choose to make a voluntary act to forgive others, just as our Heavenly Father forgave us!

Prayer

Heavenly Father,

Help me to forgive those who have injured me deeply. I cannot forgive them without Your help. If there is anyone in my life that I have not fully forgiven, call it to my attention so that I may make things right. Guard my heart so that bitterness and anger don't take root. Your Word says, "And above all things have fervent love for one another, for 'love will cover a multitude of sins" (1 Peter 4:8 NKJV). In Jesus' name, amen.

"Therefore, as God's chosen people, holy and dearly loved, clothe yourselves with compassion, kindness, humility, gentleness and patience. Bear with each other and forgive one another if any of you has a grievance against someone. Forgive as the Lord forgave you" (Colossians 3:12-13 NIV).

Day 9: God Is with His Children

"Then Joseph said to his brothers, 'Please, come near me,' and they came near. 'I am Joseph, your brother,' he said, 'the one you sold into Egypt" (Genesis 45:4 CSB).

As we pull back the curtains on the life of Joseph, we see a story that begins with suffering. Joseph's brothers hated him (Genesis 37:4) They hated him so much that they sold him into slavery (Genesis 37:28) and convinced their father that a wild animal had killed him (Genesis 37:31-33). Through their act, Joseph was sold to a man named Potiphar (Genesis 37:36) in Egypt, put in charge of his household (Genesis 39:4), but then thrown in the king's prison because Potiphar's wife falsely accused him (Genesis 39:19-20). Many years go by, but then God gave Joseph the interpretation of Pharaoh's dream, which predicted seven years of prosperity followed by seven years of famine (Genesis 41:28-29). Through God's act, Joseph was then put in charge of the entire land of Egypt, second- in-command only to Pharaoh (Genesis 41:41-43). During the famine, people from all over the world came to Egypt for grain, including Joseph's brothers. (Genesis 41:57) However, they did not know they stood before Joseph himself (Genesis 42:8).

Joseph had suffered greatly at the hands of others. Yet, despite everything he had endured, Joseph knew that God had used him to preserve, not only their lives but all the people who had found relief in the storehouses of Egypt. Throughout Joseph's troubles, God was not only with Joseph, but He blessed everything he did with success (Genesis 39:2, 21-23). Even though Joseph's brothers had meant him harm, God used their evil actions for good. In light of all that God had done in his life, Joseph chose to graciously forgive his brothers and share with them in the abundant life God had blessed him with. *Therefore, as we enlarge our perspectives within the framework of our stories within God's story, we catch our breath in wonder of the beautiful masterpiece that is God's plan of redemption.*

"And we know that God causes everything to work together for the good of those who love God and are called according to his purpose for them. For God knew his people in advance, and he chose them to become like his Son so that his Son would be the firstborn among many brothers and sisters" (Romans 8:28-29 NLT).

God was consistently working in Joseph's life when he was both second in command of Egypt and when he was thrown into prison for a crime he did not commit. God uses our individual lives and stories in ways we cannot even fathom! God transforms our stories of brokenness and pain and uses them for good. God can use your current circumstances, your past failures, and your deepest sorrows to point others to joyfully experience His love, faithfulness, and goodness. We are witnesses to His love and mercies as we go out into the world and show that despite our sufferings, we have a hope that is unshakable.

Friend, how often have you felt so empty in the past that you sideline yourself from the amazing purpose God has for you?

God welcomes us home, as He lifts us up, and He gives us a new life and calling in Christ Jesus. There is nothing you have done that exempts you from the extraordinary love God has specifically for you. God can take your greatest hardship and sorrow, and turn it into good. Most importantly, remember that God was with Joseph and He is with you today. He is always at work in the lives of His children.

Prayer

Heavenly Father,

I lay down my rags and pick up the riches You have given me in Jesus Christ, my Lord and Savior. I thank and praise You that in whatever sorrow, whatever hardship I walk through, You are with me. You alone give me the strength and confidence I need to overcome. Use every part of my life, both the good and the bad, so that others may discover the indescribable hope we have in You! A hope that does not run out or fail us, but uplifts, strengthens and encourages our hearts and our minds in Christ. Come and move in my life in a beautiful and powerful way for Your ultimate glory. In Jesus' name, amen.

"Haven't I commanded you: be strong and courageous? Do not be afraid or discouraged, for the LORD your God is with you wherever you go" (Joshua 1:9 CSB).

Day 10: A Beautiful Life in Christ

"Trust in the LORD with all your heart, And lean not on your own understanding; In all your ways acknowledge Him, And He shall direct your paths" (Proverbs 3:5-6 NKJV).

One of the greatest comforts we can have as children of God is the assurance that *everything* is in God's hands. We may be startled by the circumstances we face, but God is never surprised nor bewildered. God's timing is *perfect* in every way. What joy we have knowing that all things happen according to His perfect will. God knows all the days of our lives and He even knows every hair on our heads (Luke 12:7). Therefore, why would we worry about *anything*? We have a Heavenly Father who knows absolutely everything there is to know about us and His timing is perfect, as is His will. We may not know where we are going, but He does. He simply asks us to trust Him. He will lead us and guide us along the way, so we need not be afraid! What a beautiful joy we have when we live our lives in pursuit of God; wholeheartedly and passionately for our Savior and King!

In the kingdom of God, there are no random coincidences, no lucky chances, or whimsical fate. God's purpose will occur, for He knows the future before it happens. God is moving both in this world and in our lives, in ways we couldn't even imagine or hope for! As individuals, with only one life to live, we only get a tiny peek at all God has done and will do. Yet, God sees all things from beginning to end. God sees all things and knows all things. What a peace that settles in our hearts and minds when we trust His timing with everything. What wisdom we find when we understand that for everything there is a season. Will we not trust the One who set the stars in place (Psalm 8:3); the One who spoke and created all things (Hebrews 11:3)?

That missing piece of your life you have been desperately searching for doesn't exist in the stars, it's found in the Creator of the stars.

We can search the whole world and never be fully satisfied. Relationships, dreams, money, and jobs always have the ability to bring us happiness, but they can also bring us disappointment. Friend, the missing piece of your life you have been desperately searching for doesn't exist in the world or the stars; it's found in the Creator. Our lives here on earth are transient, but our souls are made by God for all eternity. God made it possible for us to have a personal relationship with Him through faith in Jesus Christ. In Christ, we have peace with God. We are the adopted sons and daughters of the One True King. As we walk beside our Lord and Savior, we are reminded of His loving-kindness and His mercies as He strengthens us.

"Yet God has made everything beautiful for its own time. He has planted eternity in the human heart, but even so, people cannot see the whole scope of God's work from beginning to end" (Ecclesiastes 3:11 NLT).

As human beings, made in God's image, our hearts can only be satisfied in God. Nothing on this earth could ever truly fill the desire God has placed inside our hearts. Our souls thirst for God (Psalm 42:2). When we fully fear the Lord, we completely depend on Him for everything we need, as we wholeheartedly and joyfully submit to Him as King of our lives. We worship Him in joyful gladness and a lightness of heart because He cares for our every need. With exuberance, we praise Him, not because we are made to, but out of an overabundance of thankfulness for all He has done and continues to do. How amazing is His steadfast faithfulness and love! Therefore, we know that nothing is out of place, out of sorts, or out of His control.

Prayer

Heavenly Father,
My heart's ultimate satisfaction is in You; the One who fashioned me, the One who knows everything about me! For it is when I cry out to You that my heart joyfully discovers that You have always been there, loving me and calling me by name. You never walk away from me; as You patiently extend Your invitation of grace through faith in Christ Jesus. What peace and joy my heart has discovered in You. I firmly trust that everything is in Your hands and that You are working out everything according to Your perfect timing. Show me how to trust You with all the days of my life. I come into Your presence with nothing to give and confidently thank You for all that I will receive. I don't always understand but I trust. In Jesus' name, amen.

"*As for* God, His way *is* perfect; The word of the LORD is proven; He *is* a shield to all who trust in Him" (Psalm 18:30 NKJV).

Day 11: The Armor of God

"Put on the full armor of God, so that you will be able to stand firm against the schemes of the devil. For our struggle is not against flesh and blood, but against the rulers, against the powers, against the world forces of this darkness, against the spiritual *forces* of wickedness in the heavenly *places*."

"Therefore, take up the full armor of God, so that you will be able to resist on the evil day, and having done everything, to stand firm. Stand firm therefore, having belted your waist with truth, and having put on the breastplate of righteousness, and having strapped on your feet the preparation of the gospel of peace; in addition to all, taking up the shield of faith with which you will be able to extinguish all the flaming arrows of the evil one. And take the helmet of salvation and the sword of the Spirit, which is the word of God" (Ephesians 6:11-17 NASB).

Friend, we are in a fight against our enemy, Satan. For it is Satan who tempts us into sin (1 Thessalonians 3:5) and then turns around and accuses us (Revelation 12:10). He is the father of lies (John 8:44), who prowls around like a lion looking for someone to devour (1 Peter 5:8-9). The good news is that this prowling lion has already been triumphantly defeated by the Lion of Judah (Revelation 5:5), Jesus Christ. Therefore, we must have an accurate perception of who Satan is and what he is capable of, in full light of the King of Kings, Jesus Christ. *We may be in a fight, but the war has already been won, therefore our hearts can rejoice!* Jesus defeated Satan and death when He died to the cross and rose again from the grave three days later. We have a wonderful hope of life everlasting because of Jesus' death and resurrection.

However, we must be aware of our own sinful weaknesses. Satan is not all-knowing like God and he cannot be everywhere at once. Satan does not compare to God's knowledge and understanding. But our adversary does know our vulnerabilities. He cannot see the future, but he does know the past. *He sees when we are tired or easily manipulated into our favorite temptations.* He sees our vulnerabilities when our defenses are down (being tired, hungry, or stressed), for the perfect moment to attack. Knowing this, we can use the full armor of God to stand against and resist our enemy.

Instead of giving way to Satan's arrows, stand confident in Who God is, what His Word says, and who you are in Christ. Remember, Satan is a created being (Ezekiel 28:15). He is not equal in any way to God's omnipresence, power, sovereignty, or rule. God has dominion over all of creation, including Satan. God gives us everything we need to be protected and ready to stand victorious against Satan's attacks.

Want to worry less? Pray more! Be ready and prepared with God's armor to stand against the devil and his demons. Surround yourself with the love and encouragement of other Christians who pray for you and share in your burdens. When we expose our sorrow and loneliness to the light of Christ, it robs Satan of his ability to convince us that we are all alone. Remember, you are never alone.

Prayer

Heavenly Father,
Thank You that You have given me Your Word to stand against Satan and his constant attacks against me. Strengthen me in my resistance against my adversary. Inspire me to hide Your Word in my heart so that my mouth and heart are saturated with Your Word. May it be Your Word, that overflows from my heart, and out of mouth and life, for all to see. Remind me, when I am anxious and worried, that Your Word is right there, waiting for me to open and read. Lord, guard my heart and mind and keep my thoughts steadfast in what is pleasing to You. Teach me to be always prepared and ready, especially during times when I am weak and vulnerable. My utmost desire and hope is to live today in a way that brings You glory. As Your Word says, "Beloved, do not think it strange concerning the fiery trial which is to try you, as though some strange thing happened to you; but rejoice to the extent that you partake of Christ's sufferings, that when His glory is revealed, you may also be glad with exceeding joy" (1 Peter 4:12-13 NKJV). In Jesus' name, amen.

> "You are of God, little children, and have overcome them, because He who is in you is greater than he who is in the world" (1 John 4:4 NKJV).

Day 12: In the Storm

"A great windstorm arose, and the waves were breaking over the boat, so that the boat was being swamped. He was in the stern, sleeping on the cushion. So they woke him up and said to him, 'Teacher! Don't you care that we're going to die?"

"He got up, rebuked the wind, and said to the sea, 'Silence! Be still!' The wind ceased, and there was a great calm. Then he said to them, 'Why are you afraid? Do you still have no faith?"

"And they were terrified and asked one another, 'Who then is this? Even the wind and the sea obey him" (Mark 4:37-41 CSB)!

Where do our eyes go when threatening storm clouds gather on the horizon? Where do we look when your once beautiful and bright sky turns into darkness and fear? *Our eyes look up!* The fear of life's storms is just as true today as it was for the disciples' time. We become overwhelmingly aware that we are grains of sand compared to the strength and might of the winds, waves, and the immense power that is in a single bolt of lightning. With trembling and awe, shivers go down our spines when we hear each and every thunder boom with its crack of light across the sky.

As your heart quivers and quakes at the storm's debris

surrounding you, the intensity of the aftermath may tempt you to start agonizing over circumstances of the past and start to feel fearful of the future. But don't! *Instead, turn your eyes from the struggles that surround you and look up!* Look up to the One who has everything in His hands. Look to Him who loves you, who cares for you, and who draws you to Himself in all circumstances. *When your eyes are heavy with tears,* look to Jesus. *When you are discouraged,* fix your eyes on Jesus. *When you are lacking joy,* fix your eyes on Jesus. We are in the hands of the One who simply *speaks* and the winds and the waves obey Him. We are in the sovereign hands of the One who not only made everything in all of creation but who steadfastly faithfully cares for each and every one of us. He is powerful, yet He is *kind*. He is *mighty,* yet He *cares* for you. The storm clouds may gather, but the storm will pass.

Just think friend. *If the storm had not come, would you have looked up?* Do you witness the beauty of Christ both amid blue skies and within the battery of intense storms? Even when life makes us question *who we are,* we gather strength when we look to the One who is not swayed by the winds and the waves; the One who never changes. We look to the One who made us for His glory. We look to the One who calls us His child as He gives us dignity, value, and worth. We stand firmly in the One who sees us in our personal storms of life and abundantly provides us with the strength and the perseverance to overcome them. When waves of discouragement and weariness begin to rise in your heart and mind, immerse yourself in Him both in prayer and in His Word. Dwell within the words of His love letter to you. God will never leave you or forsake you (Hebrews 13:5b NIV).

Prayer

Heavenly Father,
Thank You for Your protection in both blue skies and in the middle of life's storms. Calm the storms in my heart, so that I can be an encouragement and comfort to others going through similar squalls. Lift me up when my soul is downcast in discouragement and fear. Help me not to lose sight of You and the purpose You have for me when life's sorrows continue to batter against me. When I have lost my fervor and joy to serve the Lord, reignite my passion for You! Guide me in my current circumstances, so that instead of imploding with brokenness, I overflow with Your love, joy and peace. As the Scriptures say, "I am certain that I will see the LORD's goodness in the land of the living" (Psalm 27:13 CSB). In Jesus' name, amen.

"I lift my eyes toward the mountains. Where will my help come from? My help comes from the LORD, the Maker of heaven and earth. He will not allow your foot to slip; your Protector will not slumber. Indeed, the Protector of Israel does not slumber or sleep. The LORD protects you; the LORD is a shelter right by your side" (Psalm 121:1-5 CSB).

Day 13: He Is a Promise Keeper

"Now faith is confidence in what we hope for and assurance about what we do not see" (Hebrews 11:1 NIV).

God is calling you to boldly step out in faith and start living a life for Him. To trust Him at His Word, to trust the One who is faithful and good in whatever circumstances you face. As a believer, you already *know* His promises are true, *but is your life reflecting that reality? Are you truly trusting God?*

For many of us, there is a monumental disconnect between knowing what God says to be true and actually trusting Him at His Word. Within that gap is where our faith lies. Will the hands who lovingly knit you in your mother's womb not do what's best for you? Will you not trust the One who sees the full spectrum of your past, present, and future, to know what you need? Will you choose to trust Him even when you don't understand and are unable to see the full perspective of what He is doing for His glory? Will you confidently rest in His promises even when it *feels* like your prayers go unanswered? The Bible tells us that living in faith pleases God.

"And without faith it is impossible to please *Him*, for the one who comes to God must believe that He exists, and *that* He proves to be One who rewards those who seek Him" (Hebrews 11:6 NASB).

Imagine what you can do with faith as small as a mustard seed (Matthew 17:20 NIV). You can face seemingly impossible situations with the help of God. Every day we have the opportunity to open God's Word, meditate on His promises, and to store them up in our hearts. Just think, how can we rejoice in His promises if we never take the time to know them? His promises are true and will never fail. The Bible is overflowing with promises of God; promises we can hold on to and pray over ourselves and our loved ones. May His promises be a balm to your heart and a joy to your mind. May they give you strength, joy, and fortitude to live your day boldly and confidently in Christ. Stand firm in the promises of God, knowing that what He started in you, will be brought to completion (Philippians 1:6 NIV).

"God is not human, that he should lie, not a human being, that he should change his mind. Does he speak and then not act? Does he promise and not fulfill" (Numbers 23:19 NIV)?

The promises of God remind us of His steadfast love and faithfulness for His children. Through His promises, we see a God who loves us not because we deserve it, but because He chose to love us. *Declare God's promises aloud to remind yourself of the steadfast love we have in our Creator and King.* What a satisfaction His children find when they remember the promises of God. His Word is true and what He says will come to pass. May His Word be quick to kindle in our hearts and stop our doubts in their tracks. Hold on to His promises—every moment of the day. *Friend, stand confidently in the promises of God!*

"For no matter how many promises God has made, they are 'Yes' in Christ. And so through him the 'Amen' is spoken by us to the glory of God" (2 Corinthians 1:20 NIV).

Prayer

Heavenly Father,
I thank You that You are a God of second chances. A God of even third, fourth, and fifth chances, as You never turn me away! I am trusting You to lead me wherever You want me to go. Help me to quit striving and faithfully follow where You lead. As Isaiah said, "Here I am. Send me" (Isaiah 6:8b CSB). I'm ready to be used by You, as I know this is a prayer that will change my life. So, captivate my heart, Lord. Help me to hunger and thirst for Your Word. May I only be satisfied when I sit and soak in the pages of Your Word. Consume my heart and mind so that Your Word would nourish and feed my heart; giving it exactly what it needs to thrive. As the Psalm says, "Your word I have hidden in my heart, That I might not sin against You" (Psalm 119:11 NKJV). I trust and believe that You are already acting and moving according to Your promises. I go forward in confidence and eagerness knowing that Your promises are "yes" and "amen" in Christ. In Jesus' name, amen.

"My comfort in my suffering is this:
Your promise preserves my life"
(Psalm 119:50 NIV).

Day 14: The Empty Chair

Dearest friend, if you are sitting in the shadow of a missing loved one, know this: *God loves you. You are never alone, not for a single moment.* He sees you. He knows your pain. He knows how badly you are hurting within. He sees you in your loss, as it is amplified by the emptiness of your loved one's presence.

It's the empty chair. The empty table setting. The silence. It's all the things that remind our hearts of our loved one's absence. That it makes our hearts quake with sadness, ye*t God, in His endless mercy and grace, made a way that our Christian loved ones will not be separated from us forever.* They are at home, in the presence of Jesus, where we as believers in Christ will join them one day. What hope we have to look forward to, for in Christ, we have hope beyond the grave. When David lost his son, he said these words, "But now he is dead; why should I fast? Can I bring him back again? I shall go to him, but he shall not return to me" (2 Samuel 12:23 NKJV).

David knew that his son would not return to him here on earth, but he would be reunited with him in the life to come. *This may be hard to imagine, God's love for your loved ones is even greater than your love for them.* For it was God who formed them, who chose them before the foundation of the world (Ephesians 1:4) and loved them at the cost of His own life. Your loved ones, who have placed their hope in Jesus, have no more pain, no more death, and no more sorrow. What a joyous place they are in, with Jesus Himself.

"Now I saw a new heaven and a new earth, for the first heaven and the first earth had passed away. Also there was no more sea. Then I, John, saw the holy city, New Jerusalem, coming down out of heaven from God, prepared as a bride adorned for her husband. And I heard a loud voice from heaven saying, 'Behold, the tabernacle of God *is* with men, and they shall be His people. God Himself will be with them *and be* their God. And God will wipe away every tear from their eyes; there shall be no more death, nor sorrow, nor crying. There shall be no more pain, for the former things have passed away' (Revelation 21:1-4 NKJV).

Just as much as our hearts yearn to see their faces once again, as believers we know the best part of heaven is not just the gift of being reunited with our loved ones, but with Christ Himself! Your physical house may feel empty, but if you have Jesus, that couldn't be further from the truth. Christ is with you, right now! God promises to never leave His children and He is always right there, loving you, and providing for your every need. When you become discouraged or dismayed just look at the empty tomb, for Jesus is alive. Refresh your memory that God loved you so much that He made a way, through faith in Christ, to be fully restored to Him and live forever with Jesus. What an eternal hope we have because Jesus lives.

God has a home for His children waiting for them in heaven. Rejoice in the confidence you have that, despite these temporary sufferings, you and your Christian loved ones will spend eternity in glory with Jesus.

"So *we are* always confident, knowing that while we are at home in the body we are absent from the Lord. For we live by faith, not by sight" (2 Corinthians 5:6-7 NKJV).

Prayer

Heavenly Father,
Remind my heart that I am only a sojourner passing through this earth, as my citizenship (Philippians 3:20 NASB), is with You in heaven. Remind my grieving heart that my loved ones, who trusted in You, are now at home with Jesus. For I know that You brought them home to be with You at Your perfect timing. My heart longs for them, but I know that my loved ones have no more tears, no more pain, and no more death or suffering. They are in a place where worries and fears are a thing of the past. I thank You that You have always kept them in Your sovereign hands. For there is nothing in this life or death that is out of Your control. Keep my heart focused on the task You have set before me to joyously and abundantly live every day for You. Keep my eyes focused on sharing Your great love with as many people as I possibly can, so that they may also have the promise of eternal life. In Jesus' name, amen.

"But as it is written: 'Eye has not seen, nor ear heard,
Nor have entered into the heart of man
The things which God has prepared for those who love Him"
(1 Corinthians 2:9 NKJV).

Day 15: New Heart, New Start, New Life

"I will ask the Father, and He will give you another Helper, so that He may be with you forever; the *Helper is* the Spirit of truth, whom the world cannot receive, because it does not see Him or know *Him*; but you know Him because He remains with you and will be in you. 'I will not leave you as orphans; I am coming to you. After a little while, the world no longer *is going* to see Me, but you *are going* to see Me; because I live, you also will live. On that day you will know that I *am* in My Father, and you *are* in Me, and I in you" (John 14:16-20 NASB).

Sometimes the overwhelming ache of loneliness can persist even when we are surrounded by people. *A loneliness of heart. A loneliness of spirit.* We feel as though no one truly sees or understands the hardships we've faced. *As believers in Christ, we can be assured that we are never alone.* Not even for one moment! Because God abides in us. God in His sovereignty, may or may not take away the challenges we are facing, but you can count on the fact that He's right there with you. Loving you. Those who follow Christ are given the most amazing gift at the moment of our conversion: *the Holy Spirit.* The Holy Spirit, who lives in the heart of every believer, is with us always.

"By this we know that we remain in Him and He in us, because He has given us His Spirit. We have seen and testify that the Father has given to us His Spirit. We have seen and testify that the Father has sent the Son to *be* the Savior of the world" (1 John 4:13-14 NASB).

Jesus lovingly calls us to come follow Him, just as we are, in whatever shape or condition we are in. No matter what we have done or haven't done in the past, the precious blood of Jesus covers all of our shortcomings and sins, as we surrender our hearts and lives wholeheartedly to Him. We cheerfully hand over and entrust to Him every trouble and heartache in our lives. *The good news is that Jesus, not only meets us in our brokenness, He lovingly does not leave us how He found us.* God transforms us! He graciously gives us a new heart that seeks the desires of His heart.

"I will give you a new heart and put a new spirit within you; I will remove your heart of stone and give you a heart of flesh. I will place my Spirit within you and cause you to follow my statutes and carefully observe my ordinances" (Ezekiel 36:26-27 CSB).

Praise God, that in Christ, we are given a new heart, a new start, and a new life in Him. As children of God, we are made spiritually alive in Christ (Ephesians 2:5 NIV). Friend, if you are unsure how to take another step, remember that walking forward is simply taking one step at a time with the help of the Holy Spirit. With each step, listen and look to where He is leading you. For if we wait to go forward when we *feel* like moving, we may forever remain where we are! As *obedience to Christ precedes any feelings, thoughts, and emotions we have,* take that next step knowing the Holy Spirit is in you. You are not alone! For our

God is not a God of disorder, confusion, or bewilderment and He is not surprised by your current dilemma. He will always provide you with what you need at the proper time. He will always give you the strength to press forward, confidently knowing that He is with you.

Prayer

Heavenly Father,

At times I feel invisible, as if no one sees me in my brokenness and sorrow. But You do! You not only see me, but You are with me. Your Spirit dwells within me. May the fruit of the Spirit be evident in my life, daily conforming me into the image of Christ. For Your Word says, "But the fruit of the Spirit is love, joy, peace, patience, kindness, goodness, faithfulness, gentleness, self-control; against such things there is no law" (Galatians 5:22-23 NASB). May the evidence of the Holy Spirit, who lives in me, emanate from my heart and life in all I say and do. Spark inside my soul a renewed zest for You. I know the past is behind me and my eyes are fixed on the future, and what joyful work You have in store for me. I rejoice that You are with me every day of my life. In Jesus' name, amen.

"But when the kindness of God our Savior and *His* love for mankind appeared, He saved us, not on the basis of deeds which we did in righteousness, but in accordance with His mercy, by the washing of regeneration and renewing by the Holy Spirit, whom He richly poured out upon us through Jesus Christ our Savior, so that being justified by His grace we would be made heirs according to *the* hope of eternal life" (Titus 3:4-7 NASB).

Day 16: Living Unashamed in Christ

"Then the scribes and the Pharisees brought to Him a woman caught in adultery. And when they had set her in the midst, they said to Him, 'Teacher, this woman was caught in adultery, in the very act. Now Moses, in the law, commanded us that such should be stoned. But what do You say?' This they said, testing Him, that they might have *something* of which to accuse Him. But Jesus stooped down and wrote on the ground with *His* finger, as though He did not hear."

"So when they continued asking Him, He raised Himself up and said to them, 'He who is without sin among you, let him throw a stone at her first.' And again He stooped down and wrote on the ground. Then those who heard *it*, being convicted by *their* conscience, went out one by one, beginning with the oldest *even* to the last. And Jesus was left alone, and the woman standing in the midst. When Jesus had raised Himself up and saw no one but the woman, He said to her, 'Woman, where are those accusers of yours? Has no one condemned you?'

"She said, 'No one, Lord."

"And Jesus said to her, 'Neither do I condemn you; go and sin no more" (John 8:3-11 NKJV).

If you have grown weary and tired under the weight of your mistakes, come to Jesus. Jesus did not condemn the woman caught in adultery, and neither does He condemn you, for there is no condemnation in Christ (Romans 8:1). For in Jesus, when we ask for forgiveness, we are truly forgiven. Jesus invites you to put down the hammer and nails that you pound against your sins daily, one painful memory at a time, and let go of those regrets you have collected over the years. Friend, if you are feeling like you have wandered too far or done too much to be forgiven, know this, there is nothing that is outside of His loving mercy and forgiveness. Come to God in genuine repentance and faith, and freely live in Christ.

For in Jesus, we are free from the accusations that Satan throws in our faces to rob us of our joy. In Jesus, we are fully forgiven. Your past mistakes do not define who you are in Jesus. Friend, the beauty of the gospel is that our every sin, and all our guilt and shame, was nailed to the cross. Every single mistake we have ever made, past, present and future is forgiven through faith in Jesus. We are no longer defined by our past. *If God does not hold our sins against us, how much more should we?*

What joy we find in His extravagant grace and love! God knows every thought and every word that leaves our mouths and yet, He loves us unconditionally. God sees us at our very best and down to the darkest secrets we hide in our hearts. We are made new in Christ, living for His glory. So, live as God intended you to live; forgiven and free. "If we confess our sins, He is faithful and just to forgive us *our* sins and to cleanse us from all unrighteousness" (1 John 1:9 NKJV).

Prayer

Heavenly Father,
You know everything about me. You know my mistakes and failures. You know every word I have ever spoken and every thought in my head, and You still love me. Remind me, when I struggle to forgive myself, that Jesus' death on the cross paid for it all. Your Word says, "Therefore there is now no condemnation at all for those who are in Christ Jesus" (Romans 8:1 NASB). Teach my heart to live as a new creation in Christ, dearly loved and redeemed. As Your Word says, "For as the heavens are high above the earth, So great is His mercy toward those who fear Him; As far as the east is from the west, So far has He removed our transgressions from us" (Psalm 103:11-12 NKJV); And "Though your sins are like scarlet, They shall be as white as snow; Though they are red like crimson, They shall be as wool" (Isaiah 1:18b NKJV). I thank and praise You because I am no longer a prisoner to my sin, but have been made alive in Christ. I am set free in Jesus! In Jesus' name, amen.

"O LORD, You have searched me and known *me*. You know my sitting down and my rising up; You understand my thought afar off. You comprehend my path and my lying down, And are acquainted with all my ways. For *there is* not a word on my tongue, *But* behold, O LORD, You know it altogether. You have hedged me behind and before, And laid Your hand upon me. *Such* knowledge *is* too wonderful for me; It is high, I cannot *attain* it" (Psalm 139: 1-6 NKJV).

Day 17: A Heart of Thankfulness

"While He was on the way to Jerusalem, He was passing between Samaria and Galilee. And as He entered a village, ten men with leprosy who stood at a distance met Him; and they raised their voices, saying, 'Jesus, Master, have mercy on us!'"

"When He saw *them*, He said to them, 'Go and show yourselves to the priests.'"

"And as they were going, they were cleansed. Now one of them, when he saw that he had been healed, turned back, glorifying God with a loud voice, and he fell on his face at His feet, giving thanks to Him. And he was a Samaritan."

"But Jesus responded and said, 'Were there not ten cleansed? But the nine—where are *they*? Was no one found who returned to give glory to God, except this foreigner?' And He said to him, 'Stand up and go; your faith has made you well'" (Luke 17:11-19 NASB).

Friend, look around and see that every day you are given gifts and blessings. Today is the day you ask God for eyes that *see* this brand-new perspective with a heart that *overflows* with thankfulness. Of the ten men whose leprosy was healed by Jesus, only one overflowed with thankfulness and praise for the Healer. Take a moment, now, to put on these new glasses. Be the one that sees your current circumstances through radically different lenses than you're used to. As you look through your new glasses, you start to see things from a new perspective, a godly perspective. When you look through them, notice that your hardships and troubles automatically appear smaller, in proportion to the One who is holding you. You realize that you are in the loving hands of the One who is always faithful, always there, and always good in all He does. You start to observe things you've never noticed before. You begin to see the little mercies and miracles that were always all around us, yet you had previously failed to recognize them because of the shadows your hardships had cast upon them.

As you continue looking around, you cannot help but be filled with new hope and joy, as your heart fills with thankfulness. As you look around at all those gifts from God, your mouth cannot help but be filled with songs of praise. Your heart starts to feel overwhelmed with gratitude that had not been there before. Your circumstances still exist, but they do not feel as intimidating. Your heart, once sad, starts to feel delighted that it is no longer alone, and it is hopeful for a future in Christ.

Friend, as soon as your feet hit the floor every morning, may praise and worship be the first thing you do. Give God your *tragedies* and watch as He turns them into *songs of praise*. Give thanks to God for trials, for it is in them His providence is revealed. Our God is a personal God. He is a God who cares for and pays attention to every tiny detail of our lives. As believers in Christ, we are to count our trials as a joy!

"Consider it pure joy, my brothers and sisters, whenever you face trials of many kinds, because you know that the testing of your faith produces perseverance. Let perseverance finish its work so that you may be mature and complete, not lacking anything" (James 1:2-4 NIV).

Prayer

Heavenly Father,
Your Word says,

"Make a joyful shout to the LORD, all you lands!
Serve the LORD with gladness; Come before His presence with singing. Know that the LORD, He *is* God; *It is* He who has made us, and not we ourselves; *We are* His people and the sheep of His pasture. Enter into His gates with thanksgiving, *And* into His courts with praise.
Be thankful to Him, *and* bless His name.
For the LORD *is* good; His mercy *is* everlasting,
And His truth *endures* to all generations" (Psalm 100 NKJV). In Jesus' name, amen.

"Rejoice always, pray without ceasing, in everything give thanks; for this is the will of God for you in Christ Jesus" (1 Thessalonians 5:16-18 NASB).

Day 18: In Wonderment and Awe

"The heavens declare the glory of God, and the expanse proclaims the work of his hands. Day after day they pour out speech; night after night they communicate knowledge. There is no speech; there are no words; their voice is not heard. Their message has gone out to the whole earth, and their words to the ends of the world. In the heavens he has pitched a tent for the sun. It is like a bridegroom coming from his home; it rejoices like an athlete running a course. It rises from one end of the heavens and circles to their other end; nothing is hidden from its heat" (Psalm 19:1-6 CSB).

Gaze up and marvel at the night sky, with its beauty displayed in the countless number of stars. *Have you ever been in awe of its vast allure or frightened by its power?* When thunder cracks through the sky and lightning electrifies the heavens, does your spine shiver with the thought that there is Someone bigger than you that created this magnificent sky? God is the Creator of all things. Look and be astonished. What joy it should bring us as we gaze upon creation and stand in awe of our Creator. We gasp at the beauty and wonderment of all He has lovingly made. From the trees, flowers, birds, and bees to the majestic backdrop of the mountains and the crystal blue waters of the sea, we are in awe. Just look at your own uniqueness and design. Look at your toes, stretch out your hands! You were no accident, but intentionally, lovingly, and intricately designed by God. "So God created mankind in His *own* image, in the image of God he created them; male and female he created them" (Genesis 1:27 NIV).

The entire universe displays the splendor of His handiwork. God spoke into existence each and every creature, from the tiny ant to the mighty lion. All have a purpose and were made to bring their Creator glory! The world that was once perfect, was broken because of sin. It was only after Adam and Eve disobeyed God, that the ground was cursed (Genesis 3:17-18).

"Against its will, all creation was subjected to God's curse. But with eager hope, the creation looks forward to the day when it will join God's children in glorious freedom from death and decay. For we know that all creation has been groaning as in the pains of childbirth right up to the present time" (Romans 8:20-22 NLT).

We see the effects of sin's curse both in ourselves and in all of creation. Our ability to perceive that something is not right in the world and within ourselves was given to us by God when His law was written on our hearts (Romans 2:14-15). God has gifted us with a conscience. *A conscience to perceive within our very hearts the brokenness in ourselves and in this world.* The Good News is that God didn't leave us in our brokenness! God created a rescue plan to restore mankind to Himself, which could only be carried out by the perfect Lamb of God, His sacrifice in our place! As Jesus entered humanity, fully God and fully man, He paid for our sins and redeemed us from the law's curse with His death on the cross (Galatians 3:13). God revealed this beautiful plan of redemption in His Word; a love letter written to us that shows the full story of God's extravagant love and grace. "The Word became flesh and dwelt among us. We observed his glory, the glory as the one and only Son from the Father, full of grace and truth" (John 1:14 CSB).

Prayer

Heavenly Father,
I look up to the heavens and gasp in wonder! Your handiwork surrounds me, both in nature and in my heart. Your Word says, "For every house is built by someone, but God is the builder of everything" (Hebrews 3:4 NIV). Thank You that You have given us all we need to believe. Thank You for the gift of my conscience as my heart is awakened by You drawing me to You. I thank You that in Your Word we find the way to eternal life through faith in Jesus. I look forward, in earnest hope and expectation, to when all the earth will be made new. In Jesus' name, amen.

"They know the truth about God because he has made it obvious to them. For ever since the world was created, people have seen the earth and sky. Through everything God made, they can clearly see his invisible qualities—his eternal power and divine nature. So they have no excuse for not knowing God" (Romans 1:19-20 NLT).

Day 19: Living Victoriously in Christ

"What, then, shall we say in response to these things? If God is for us, who can be against us? He who did not spare his own Son, but gave him up for us all—how will he not also, along with him, graciously give us all things? Who will bring any charge against those whom God has chosen? It is God who justifies. Who then is the one who condemns? No one. Christ Jesus who died—more than that, who was raised to life—is at the right hand of God and is also interceding for us. Who shall separate us from the love of Christ? Shall trouble or hardship or persecution or famine or nakedness or danger or sword? As it is written: 'For your sake we face death all day long; we are considered as sheep to be slaughtered.''

"No, in all these things we are more than conquerors through him who loved us. For I am convinced that neither death nor life, neither angels nor demons, neither the present nor the future, nor any powers, neither height nor depth, nor anything else in all creation, will be able to separate us from the love of God in Christ Jesus our Lord" (Romans 8:31-39 NIV).

Child of God, if you are feeling discouraged, disheartened, or drained from the circumstances you are facing, know this: God is for you! God is not against you. Not even for a second. When you feel alone and unsure of His love for you, remember that *no one* and *nothing* can separate you from His love. *Absolutely nothing.* As you read these truths, let them grab hold of you and never leave you the same. Two thousand years ago, God's rescue plan of salvation was accomplished in Jesus' death and resurrection. Because Christ lives, we have life everlasting! Christ's arrival into Jerusalem was humbly on the back of a donkey (Matthew 21:5), but He will return on a white horse (Revelation 19:11). The same Jesus who was mocked, beaten, and given a crown of thorns will one day have every knee bow and every tongue will confess Him as Lord (Philippians 2:10-11 NKJV).

Hide these powerful truths in your heart and in your mind. When you are lonely, in a hospital bed, or facing the death of a loved one; remember that God loves you, *nothing can separate you from His love. Just as death could not keep its grasp over Jesus, don't let anything in this life hold its power over you.* In Christ, break free of whatever has a clutch over you. Fight the fight against Satan and sin. Don't place limits on yourself and what you can do through the power of Christ. *Where your strength lacks, His power abounds.* Just as Christ defeated the stronghold of sin and death, you have the freedom to defeat whatever is in your life that has you in bondage. As a believer, you have the power of God living inside of you, so go forward in confidence knowing that you can overcome whatever area Satan attacks. In Christ, we are set free, as He gives us the power to let loose every chain of guilt, fear, and sin that holds us down. When you feel overwhelmed, take whatever hardship you face and put it in the light of Christ. When all you can see is failure and defeat, ask God to give you a perspective where you see all things as an overcomer.

The foundation of our faith is firmly built on Christ, our living hope (1 Peter 1:3). As believers we can find great encouragement that the Word of God has stood true against the backdrop of time and critics. The message of the cross speaks to us across the space of time to tell us that the work is finished. That we simply need to trust in Jesus.

"It is this Good News that saves you if you continue to believe the message I told you—unless, of course, you believed something that was never true in the first place. I passed on to you what was most important and what had also been passed on to me. Christ died for our sins, just as the Scriptures said. He was buried, and he was raised from the dead on the third day, just as the Scriptures said" (1 Corinthians 15:2-4 NLT).

Prayer

Heavenly Father,
I rejoice that the tomb is empty! Christ lives, therefore I also live through faith in Him. I thank You that in Jesus there is life; life eternal. My heart rejoices and is glad in You. In Jesus' name, amen.

"Why are you seeking the living One among the dead? He is not here, but He has risen. Remember how He spoke to you while He was still in Galilee, saying that the Son of Man must be handed over to sinful men, and be crucified, and on the third day rise *from the dead*" (Luke 24:5b-7 NASB).

Day 20: The Great Exchange

"Give all your worries and cares to God, for he cares about you" (1 Peter 5:7 NLT).

Friend, give God your *sorrows*, your *bitterness*, your *tragedies*, your *anger*, your *guilt*, your *losses*, your *brokenness*, your *anxieties*, your *disappointments*, your *worry*, and your *unforgiveness*. As you surrender to Him all your heartaches, lay down your burdens at the feet of Jesus, the Savior who loves you and cares for you more than you could ever imagine! In this world, we will have trouble (John 16:33 NIV). Yet, Jesus gives us the most extraordinary gift of all. He gives us peace that is not of this world. As we give Jesus every worry, anxiety, trouble and fear; Jesus gives us His peace. "And the peace of God, which surpasses all understanding, will guard your hearts and minds in Christ Jesus" (Philippians 4:7 CSB). In Jesus, find the peace your soul desires. *Friend, come to Jesus from wherever you are, just as you are in this moment.* You don't have to hold the weight of your burdens by yourself any more, simply give them all to Jesus.

"Jesus said, 'I am leaving you with a gift—peace of mind and heart. And the peace I give is a gift the world cannot give. So don't be troubled or afraid" (John 14:27 NLT).

Friend, it is when we humble ourselves before God that we can start to let go of all of our heartaches and allow God to replace them with His joy and peace. God desires to know what is in our hearts, He is never too busy to listen or speak when we come before Him with a sincere heart. It is in our humility, that we realize our need for God and admit that we are unable to carry everything ourselves. We need to accept God's strength, wisdom, and comfort daily and the wonderful news is that God is more than willing to give us those things. He is a generous Heavenly Father, abounding with love, and is waiting to give to His children who come to Him and ask.

In the middle of your sorrow, in your time of need, cry out to your Heavenly Father. Pour out your burdens and suffering to the Lord. Don't keep your mouth and heart closed in silence but empty all your burdens into His hands. Cry out to God at the top of your lungs, telling Him all about your sorrows, fears, and shattered dreams. He will always meet you in your time of need. "Cast your burden on the LORD, and he will sustain you; he will never allow the righteous to be shaken" (Psalm 55:22 CSB).

It is because He knows what we are going through,
that we cry out to Jesus.
In the middle of a cancer diagnosis, call out to Jesus.
When you are facing your biggest fear, call out to Jesus.
When life drains you of joy, call out to Jesus.
He will give you the *strength* you have been lacking.
He will give you the *peace* you have been seeking.
He will give you the *hope* you have been searching for.
He gives His children, *life* everlasting.

Prayer

Heavenly Father,
I give You all my worries, discouragements, anxieties, brokenness, sorrows, fears, unforgiveness, finances, addictions, self-criticism, my health, my family, my nightmares of the past, and the hopes and dreams of my future. I place everything that is weighing me down; into the nail pierced hands of Jesus so willingly stretched out onto the cross, giving His very life for me. Thank You that I am not meant to carry the cares of the world on my shoulders, as only You can. In Jesus' name, amen.

> "Do you not know? Have you not heard?
> The LORD is the everlasting God,
> the Creator of the ends of the earth.
> He will not grow tired or weary,
> and his understanding no one can fathom.
> He gives strength to the weary and
> increases the power of the weak.
> Even youths grow tired and weary,
> and young men stumble and fall;
> but those who hope in the LORD will renew their strength.
> They will soar on wings like eagles;
> they will run and not grow weary,
> they will walk and not be faint" (Isaiah 40:28-31 NIV).

Day 21: Bursting with Joy

"In the same region, shepherds were staying out in the fields and keeping watch at night over their flock. Then an angel of the Lord stood before them, and the glory of the Lord shone around them, and they were terrified. But the angel said to them, 'Don't be afraid, for look, I proclaim to you good news of great joy that will be for all the people: Today in the city of David a Savior was born for you, who is the Messiah, the Lord. This will be the sign for you: You will find a baby wrapped tightly in cloth and lying in a manger."

"Suddenly there was a multitude of the heavenly host with the angel, praising God and saying:"

"Glory to God in the highest heaven, and peace on earth to people he favors" (Luke 2:8-14 CSB)!

That very first Christmas, the love of God came down from heaven. The heavenly hosts' announcement of the birth of the Messiah, reminds us that the inexpressible joy of Christ is a joy unlike anything of this world. Friend, there is a difference between our happiness and joy! Happiness treats us like a roller coaster, jilting us up and down and every which way. Our happiness is solely dependent on our circumstances and mood. Whereas our joy is in Christ, and it lasts for all of eternity. *For the hope of the gospel shines bright in a world full of pain and suffering.* Christ is the lasting joy our hearts have been seeking; His love is unconditional.

God's loving kindness and faithfulness toward you do not change or fade based on the highs and lows of the circumstances you face. When you are up on the mountaintop, He doesn't love you any more or any less than when you are traveling through valleys. Friend, know this, God is always good. Your circumstances may change, but God never will. "Jesus Christ *is* the same yesterday, today, and forever" (Hebrews 13:8 NKJV). For when we begin to grasp the truth that God's goodness never changes, what peace and joy our hearts discover! In the beginning, God created all things, and all things were good (Genesis 1:31). His goodness is alive and all around us! "Every good and perfect gift is from above, coming down from the Father of lights, who does not change like shifting shadows" (James 1:17 CSB).

Whatever the circumstances, worship God! We joyfully come and adore the King of heaven and earth, and not just on Christmas, but every day. Daily we lay down our troubles at His feet in worship, and delightfully treasure the gifts of peace and hope He so graciously offers us. May our lives exude exaltation for King Jesus, as we overflow with excitement, fervor, and joy for the One who gave His life as the ultimate sacrifice. In whatever messiness that surrounds you, lift your hands in praise to your Provider, your Deliverer, your Rock, your Refuge, your Hope, and your Salvation. As your praise goes up to heaven, welcome His joy and peace to fill your heart and every fiber of your being. Richly live each and every day because it is a precious gift given specifically to you from God who loves you!

When you are surrounded by blessings, praise God, for He loves you! When you are facing life's hardships and troubles, praise God, for He loves you! When your heart is burdened with sorrow, praise God, because He is for you! Fill your heart with joy and praise because you know that God is good (Psalm 34:8). We rejoice because our God is holy (Isaiah 6:3). We rejoice because our God is just (Deuteronomy 32:4). We rejoice because our God is merciful (Ephesians 2:4-5). We rejoice because our God is faithful (2 Timothy 2:13).

Prayer

Heavenly Father,
Remind my heart when it is lonely and sad, that it is never alone! You are always with me. I know Your Word says, "Therefore the LORD himself will give you a sign: The virgin shall conceive and give birth to a son, and will call him Immanuel" (Isaiah 7:14 NIV). I thank and praise You that through faith in Jesus, my life has been changed forever! Train my heart to be cheerful and glad in all circumstances. I praise You for the cornucopia of blessings You shower down from heaven all around me! Put a song of praise in my heart and on my lips. All praise and honor to You. In Jesus' name, amen.

> "For a Child will be born to us, a Son will be given to us; And the government will rest on His shoulders; And His name will be called Wonderful Counselor, Mighty God, Eternal Father, Prince of Peace" (Isaiah 9:6 NASB).

Day 22: Even If

"Look!' Nebuchadnezzar shouted. 'I see four men, unbound, walking around in the fire unharmed! And the fourth looks like a god!"

"Then Nebuchadnezzar came as close as he could to the door of the flaming furnace and shouted: 'Shadrach, Meshach, and Abednego, servants of the Most High God, come out! Come here!"

"So Shadrach, Meshach, and Abednego stepped out of the fire. Then the high officers, officials, governors, and advisers crowded around them and saw that the fire had not touched them. Not a hair on their heads was singed, and their clothing was not scorched. They didn't even smell of smoke!"

"Then Nebuchadnezzar said, 'Praise to the God of Shadrach, Meshach, and Abednego! He sent his angel to rescue his servants who trusted in him. They defied the king's command and were willing to die rather than serve or worship any god except their own God. Therefore, I will make this decree: If any people, whatever their race or nation or language, speak a word against the God of Shadrach, Meshach, and Abednego, they will be torn limb from limb, and their houses will be turned into heaps of rubble. There is no god who can rescue like this" (Daniel 3:25-29 NLT)!

These three courageous three men defied the king when they refused to worship anything or anyone but God Almighty, our true King! They were unrelenting in their faith as they stared death in the face and defied Nebuchadnezzar.

"Shadrack, Meshach, and Abednego replied, "O Nebuchadnezzar, we do not need to defend ourselves before you. If we are thrown into the blazing furnace, the God whom we serve is able to save us. He will rescue us from your power, Your Majesty. But even if he doesn't, we want to make it clear to you, Your Majesty, that we will never serve your gods or worship the gold statue you have set up" (Daniel 3:16-18 NLT).

Each of these men was willing to go to their death rather than renounce their faith. They defiantly declared to the ungodly king that *"even if"* God did not save them, they would never worship anyone, but Him alone. However, we are called to boldly and joyfully live our faith every single moment of our lives, as we fix our eyes on Jesus. That's the beauty of the joy Christians have in Christ. We have everlasting hope and an unshakeable peace in Christ. We are called to confidently live, not as our culture tells us to live, but how God has revealed to us in His Word. Today, decide to trust *God*, in the *"even if..."*

> Stand up for Christ, *even if* we are laughed at
> or ostracized for our faith in Jesus.
> Share your faith, *even if* you are nervous
> or don't know what to say.
> Thank God, *even if* we lose our job.
> Worship God, *even if* the cancer doesn't go away.
> Praise God, *even if* our loved one passes away from a
> terminal illness.

Prayer

Heavenly Father,

As Your child, I thank and praise You that You chose me. Inspire me to courageously and boldly live my faith through the help of the Holy Spirit inside my heart. Fill me to overflowing, Holy Spirit! May my words and actions be filled with kindness, goodness, and love so that others may see the hope of Christ living bright in me. Encourage my heart, when I face difficult circumstances so that even in hardships, I can express the joy and confidence that comes from You. My eyes are continually on You, *even if* the thing that I most fear happens. I *know* that You are always with me, therefore I will not be afraid. In Jesus' name, amen.

"Therefore we do not lose heart, but though our outer person is decaying, yet our inner *person* is being renewed day by day. For our momentary, light affliction is producing for us an eternal weight of glory far beyond all comparison, while we look not at the things which are seen, but at the things which are not seen; for the things which are seen are temporal, but the things which are not seen are eternal" (2 Corinthians 4:16-18 NASB).

Day 23: Don't Forget the Wilderness

"Remember that the LORD your God led you on the entire journey these forty years in the wilderness, so that he might humble you and test you to know what was in your heart, whether or not you would keep his commands. He humbled you by letting you go hungry; then he gave you manna to eat, which you and your ancestors had not known, so that you might learn that man does not live on bread alone but on every word that comes from the mouth of the Lord. Your clothing did not wear out, and your feet did not swell these forty years. Know in mind that the LORD your God has been disciplining you just as a man disciplines his son. So keep the commands of the Lord your God by walking in his ways and fearing him" (Deuteronomy 8:2-6 CSB).

Through a miraculous display of God's power and might, God delivered the Israelites from slavery in Egypt, rescuing them from their bondage to the Egyptians (Exodus 20:2). For the next 40 years, God faithfully led them through the wilderness and into the Promise Land; as He lovingly provided for their every need along the way. Their clothes and their sandals never wore out (Deuteronomy 29:5 CSB), and God daily supplied food to sustain them. Despite all God had done to provide for their every need, the Israelites constantly wavered in their faith and trust. We, like the Israelites, see that God provides for us daily. We remember how He has faithfully taken care of us in the past, and yet we still question whether God loves us. We question His faithfulness and His providence in our lives. We waver in our faith. But God, in His unfailing love, takes care of our every need again and again.

We all go through times in our lives that act as a spiritual wilderness experience. As believers, we are on a Christian journey that begins with our rebirth into the family of God. We will face many obstacles and challenges, but if we release them into God's hands, He will use them to make us more like Christ. As we learn to follow our Savior, through both the valleys and on the mountaintops, our eyes start to see God in a whole new way! Each step we take starts to make deep tread marks of faith, marking our times of deep dependence on God in our hearts and lives. These beautiful marks serve as reminders of His love and faithfulness so that in the future, our instinct will be to stay close to our Provider and Comforter. As we walk with the Lord in all our circumstances, we rejoice in our humility and in our dependence on the One who provides everything we need. *What assurances we have knowing that He carried us through the heartache in the past, He will do it again in the future!* May we never forget God's providence for His children, both in the good times and in the seasons that put our faith to the test.

Often, it is not until we get to the other side of our troubles that we see all God has done in that time of suffering and pain. Had He not taken us through our times of trouble, our hearts wouldn't have experienced the strength, hope, comfort, and encouragement God gives us in the middle of the chaos. His handiwork was written all over our lives; in the ways He taught us humility, patience, dependence, discipline, thankfulness, and a love for His Word. What love the Father has for us! Let your heart be filled with indescribable gladness at His constant faithfulness and tender loving care for you.

Prayer

Heavenly Father,

Help me to never forget! Consistently remind my heart of how You have faithfully guided me and provided for me every step of the way. The road has not always been easy, yet You have protected me by being my staff and my shield. You have comforted me in times of deep sorrow and discouragement. Continually call to my mind the sweetness of our time together in life's valleys. It was there that I saw You in a way that has transformed my life completely. It was there that I learned to rely on You. Encourage my heart not to forget Your abundant mercies when I am settled and satisfied. Lord, I thank You for my time of suffering, for it was there that I truly met You. In Jesus' name, amen.

"When you have eaten and are satisfied, you shall bless the LORD your God for the good land which He has given you. Be careful that you do not forget the LORD your God by failing to keep His commandments, His ordinances, and His statutes which I am commanding you today; otherwise, when you eat and are satisfied, and you build good houses and live *in them*, and when your herds and your flocks increase, and your silver and gold increase, and everything that you have increases, then your heart will become proud and you will forget the LORD your God who brought you out of the land of Egypt, out of the house of slavery" (Deuteronomy 8:10-14 NASB).

Day 24: Passionately Following Jesus

"Jesus went out again beside the sea. The whole crowd was coming to him, and he was teaching them. Then, passing by, he saw Levi the son of Alphaeus sitting at the tax office, and he said to him, 'Follow me,' and he got up and followed him."

"While he was reclining at the table in Levi's house, many tax collectors and sinners were eating with Jesus and his disciples, for there were many who were following him. When the scribes who were Pharisees saw that he was eating with sinners and tax collectors, they asked his disciples, 'Why does he eat with tax collectors and sinners?'"

"When Jesus heard this, he told them, 'It is not those who are well who need a doctor, but those who are sick. I didn't come to call the righteous, but sinners" (Mark 2:13-17 CSB).

Friend, Jesus is calling you, to come and follow Him. Jesus calls every man, woman, and child from every culture and nation on earth to follow Him and to know Him personally. God calls His sons and daughters by their name, for we are His (John 10:3). We *do not* follow Jesus because it is easy; Jesus told us that on this earth, we will face troubles (John 16:33 NIV). We *do not* follow Jesus for riches on this earth; Jesus tells us that our treasure is in heaven (Matthew 6:19-21). *Friend, we follow Jesus because in Him our sins are fully forgiven.* "Jesus answered, 'I am the way and the truth and the life. No one comes to the Father except through me" (John 14:6 NIV).

Just think, what if the trouble you are enduring is a gift from God, allowing you to see more clearly your desperate need for Him? What if God used your deepest sorrow to open your heart and mind to your need for a Savior? Would not enduring temporary hardships be worth an eternity secured with Jesus? When we come to Jesus in genuine repentance and faith, God welcomes us home with arms wide open and compassionately forgives us for all the things we have done. He invites us out of our brokenness and into a brand-new life in Him! It doesn't matter what we have done or haven't done, God pursues each of His sons and daughters because He loves us.

As followers of Christ, we joyfully surrender our lives to the One True King! Holding nothing back, we passionately and fervently live "all in" for Christ! *God created our souls to exist eternally and what we do in this life has an eternal impact.* We must ask ourselves, would our Heavenly Father be glorified in how I am living? Friend, whether you are a teacher, a nurse, a business professional, a student, a retiree, a lawyer, a parent, or a grandparent, be the very best at whatever you do for God's glory. *Be such a bright light and kind heart as you do whatever God has placed you to do, that others ask the reason for your Hope, the reason why you are so different from the rest of the world.* Use whatever your passion, talent, or skill God has gifted you to reach others with the hope you have in Christ. When we live our lives to bring God glory and honor, we are bright lights of hope pointing others to the eternal life found in Christ.

"Therefore, whether you eat or drink, or whatever you do, do all to the glory of God" (1 Corinthians 10:31 NKJV).

Prayer

Heavenly Father,
Your Word says, "What man of you, having a hundred sheep, if he loses one of them, does not leave the ninety-nine in the wilderness, and go after the one which is lost until he finds it? And when he has found *it*, he lays *it* on his shoulders, rejoicing. And when he comes home, he calls together *his* friends and neighbors, saying to them, 'Rejoice with me, for I have found my sheep which was lost!' I say to you that likewise there will be more joy in heaven over one sinner who repents than over ninety-nine just persons who need no repentance" (Luke 15:4-7 NKJV). Thank You that You leave the *ninety-nine* for the *one*! Thank You that You put the lost on Your shoulders to bring them home, rejoicing. What love You have for Your children. In Jesus' name, amen.

"Then Jesus said to His disciples, 'If anyone desires to come after Me, let him deny himself, and take up his cross, and follow Me. For whoever desires to save his life will lose it, but whoever loses his life for My sake will find it. For what profit is it to a man if he gains the whole world, and loses his own soul? Or what will a man give in exchange for his soul" (Matthew 16:24-26 NKJV)?

Day 25: Don't Mind the Mess

"I give thanks to my God for every remembrance of you, always praying with joy for all of you in my every prayer, because of your partnership in the gospel from the first day until now. I am sure of this, that he who started a good work in you will carry it on to completion until the day of Christ Jesus" (Philippians 1:3-6 CSB).

Friend, we live in a society that loves to throw things away. When an appliance breaks, we buy a new one. If our car gets old, we trade it in for a newer model. If our relationship falls apart, we find someone new. Yet, when many of us have suffered and struggled through hardships that have left us broken and crushed in spirit, God doesn't throw us out. He *welcomes us in our brokenness and wants to restore, heal, and renew our hearts like never before.* The rest of the world may want to pass right by us, but God never will. Instead, He welcomes us into a restored relationship with Himself. We were made to have a life of peace, hope, and joy in Christ!

You, yes you, are precious in the sight of God! God cares about every crease and crack that has happened to your heart. He knows every challenge you have faced, down to your deepest pain and sorrows. As children of God, we know that in this life, we are not exempt from troubles or loss. There is nothing we can do to avoid them nor is there a way to remove them from our lives, yet God can use them to shape us to be more like Christ.

The work of being shaped can be a messy process, as there is refining, molding, and healing take place. However, when we allow God to work in us to grow and mature our faith, the ugliness of our situation reshapes into beauty in our lives. It is in these moments that we have to choose to take our eyes off the mess and keep our eyes on Christ. We can rejoice that despite our challenges, God is using these times to produce in us a heart that overflows with kindness, patience, generosity, love, empathy, and understanding for those around us.

"Therefore, since we have been justified by faith, we have peace with God through our Lord Jesus Christ. We have also obtained access through him by faith into this grace in which we stand, and we boast in the hope of the glory of God. And not only that, but we also boast in our afflictions, because we know that affliction produces endurance, endurance produces proven character, and proven character produces hope. This hope will not disappoint us, because God's love has been poured out in our hearts through the Holy Spirit who was given to us" (Romans 5:1-5 CSB).

As we begin to see God more clearly in our troubles and circumstances, it shines a light on the attributes of His love, faithfulness, and mercy that we had not seen before. Friends, each and every one of us were made to know God and to be known personally by Him. We can either allow our circumstances to draw us closer to God, as He molds and shapes our hearts, or allow them to callous our hearts, becoming more bitter and discouraged by the hardships we have endured. God cares about our hearts and He cares about the shaping of our character. Praise God that it is in our times of trouble, that we know Him deeper still. Therefore, as His children, we are *not exempt nor excused* from life's hardships; n*or are we surprised or dismayed* by the troubles we face. As Christians, we joyfully face whatever circumstance or trial that faces us with the confidence we have in Christ.

Prayer

Heavenly Father,
I rejoice that I am a work in progress and that You have promised to finish Your work in me. I know that it is often in the middle of the mess, that You are doing beautiful and wondrous work in my life. A work that I can take joy in. For You don't give up on me! Thank You that You restore, renew, and heal our brokenness and transform our lives into a brilliant light, shining for Christ. As Your Word says, "In the same way, let your light shine before others, that they may see your good deeds and glorify your Father in heaven" (Matthew 5:16 NIV). Help me to shine bright, Lord! May my life radiate with the hope and joy I have found in You. In Jesus' name, amen.

> "For we are God's masterpiece.
> He has created us anew in Christ Jesus,
> so we can do the good things he planned for us long ago"
> (Ephesians 2:10 NLT).

Day 26: Like a Child

"Be anxious for nothing, but in everything by prayer and supplication, with thanksgiving, let your requests be made known to God; and the peace of God, which surpasses all understanding, will guard your hearts and minds through Christ Jesus" (Philippians 4:6-7 NKJV).

Sometimes the only words we can manage to mutter are, ***"Help me, Father!"*** Though those precious words may be the only ones our hurting hearts can muster, we know He hears us. When we cry out to God with sincere hearts, genuinely seeking Him, we know He hears and answers our heart's deepest cry. Trust the Creator of the universe, who knows everything about you from past to future, to provide you with everything you need at His good and perfect time.

May our joy overflow within us, like a child who eagerly awaits all day to tell their dad about their day, as we lay bare an account of all that is on our hearts and minds to our Heavenly Father. We voice our thanksgivings, adorations, and praises to the Maker of the universe, the Author of life itself. What a priceless gift we have been given by our Heavenly Father! God's Word tells us to, "pray without ceasing" (1 Thessalonians 5:17 NASB), that we are called to eagerly cry out to our Heavenly Father night and day, in the middle of life's storm, as well as in the sunshine of our greatest joys and triumphs. We are invited to spend time with the One who never sleeps and never turns us away. We simply come to Him at any hour of the day.

Prayer is not a mix of grandiose words and empty phrases, but the earnest seeking of our Heavenly Father with our hearts and souls. In prayer, take the burdens you carry and lay them down, bare, before our Father. Our Father is faithful and good. No longer will you struggle under the weight of your burden, when you fervently and persistently lay them down before Him. So often we may feel alone, with the false assumption that no one wants to hear the burdens of our hearts and minds. Yet this couldn't be further from the truth, it is on our knees that we discover what we were looking for all along, God Himself. Encounter the God of the universe who wants to hear from you. The One who holds all things in His hands, and desires to talk with His children as intimately and as tenderly as a child talking to their father. Rest in the assurance that God hears every word, for He passionately loves and cares for you.

As a child of God, our hearts crave uninterrupted time with our Heavenly Father. For we have the inexpressible privilege and honor that we can speak directly to our Father who is in heaven. There is nothing too small that He will not care about, nor anything too big that you cannot tell Him. Friend, continue lifting up what burdens your heart, praying for others, as well as thanking and praising Him for all His goodness, grace, and mercy. God already knows what you are going through and the hardships you have endured, yet He still wants to hear it from you! *Prayer is a precious time that not only changes our lives but has the power to change the world around us.* Prayer is often the thing we do the least, yet it holds the greatest power because of

Whom we have access to, through Jesus Christ our Savior. God is a Father who loves His children deeply, and He desires for us to come to Him to unload our burdens and experience His peace.

Prayer

Heavenly Father,

Help me! For I lack the words to say right now. Surround me with Your compassionate love! You know how my heart is prone to discouragement, as I have cried a thousand tears. I am sorry that I often wait until my time of need to rediscover how You have been there all along. I thank You that in times of sorrow, Your love blankets my heart and soothes my soul. You are the love that I feel in my heart and You are closer than the warmth of the sun on my skin. Restore my confidence and hope that I might burst with joy again. Help me to rely on You like a little child, aware of my own spiritual vulnerability and helplessness. Renew my strength and encourage my heart to follow You when my soul is disheartened. Thank You that You have adopted me as Your child so that I can cry out to You. In Jesus' name, amen.

"The *righteous* cry out, and the LORD hears And rescues them from all their troubles. The LORD is near to the brokenhearted And saves those who are crushed in spirit. The afflictions of the righteous are many, But the LORD rescues him from them all" (Psalm 34:17-19 NASB).

Day 27: You Are Called to Encourage

"And let us consider how we may spur one another on toward love and good deeds, not giving up meeting together, as some are in the habit of doing, but encouraging one another—and all the more as you see the Day approaching" (Hebrews 10:24-25 NIV).

As believers in Christ, every one of us is called to inspire each other, as we build each other up as a family of believers. What joy and cheer we receive when we are all together, united in our worship of the One True King. Yet, people who make up the church struggle with sin, just like all of humanity. Christians are not exempt from worldly hardships, sorrows, divisions, misunderstandings, and disagreements. The family of God consists of *individuals who are broken, hurting, and in desperate need of a Savior.* Keep in mind, churches are made up of sinful people with faults of their own who desire to be more like Christ. *Only* God is perfect. It can be incredibly easy to become disappointed or disillusioned from attending a church, and it can be even easier to just want to walk away and give up on ever finding that "perfect church". Sometimes the weight of our discouragement is so heavy, it causes us to disconnect from other believers altogether.

Friend, no one is perfect and we all come to church as we are. God has given every follower of Christ gifts, to be used in encouragement to others. *The question we should be asking ourselves is not "What should I be getting out of meeting with other believers?" but "How can I serve and be encouraging to them?"* We need *to be able to give*, as well *as receive*. We have the joy of sharing words of hope, blessings, and life, with those around us. Together, we live to cheer on and inspire one another in our walk with the Lord. Church is not about a physical brick and mortar building, it's about believers coming together to worship God.

"They were continually devoting themselves to the apostles' teaching and to fellowship, to the breaking of bread and to prayer. Everyone kept feeling a sense of awe; and many wonders and signs were taking place through the apostles. And all the believers were together and had all things in common; and they would sell their property and possessions and share them with all, to the extent that anyone had need. Day by day continuing with one mind in the temple, and breaking bread from house to house, they were taking their meals together with gladness and sincerity of heart, praising God and having favor with all the people. And the Lord was adding to their number day by day those who were being saved" (Acts 2:42-47 NASB).

As Christians, we pray for the same passion to share the gospel as well as the ability to love others, as the early followers of Christ so beautifully displayed. How can we not but be motivated to share our faith and gather as believers? It is when we are burdened that we need to be around people more than ever. We need to receive their encouragement and presence in our lives, so we can be with others in their sorrow, providing the comfort and compassion that others have shown us. God made us to live in a relationship with Him and with one another. We have the joy of sharing our dinner tables but we also share our sorrows, as we lift up, pray for, and encourage one another in all seasons of life.

Today, ask Him for His guidance and blessing to be used in a mighty way in your life, in the lives of believers, and those in the world. Remember, attending church is not what makes you a follower of Christ, but whether you are trusting in Jesus. *Christians make a decision to receive Jesus personally as their Lord and Savior, trusting that His death paid for all their sins in full and that through His resurrection there is the promise of eternal life.* There may very well be someone sitting to your left or your right, who doesn't truly *know Jesus.* If so, just think: you were put there, at this very moment, to show them the love of Christ and share with them the reason for your hope.

Prayer

Heavenly Father,
You remind us of Your compassionate love for the Church. A love so great that Christ gave His life so that we might have everlasting life with Him. You know me better than I know myself, Lord. You know I tend to withdraw and retreat in isolation, but You pull me out of my solitude and into the fellowship of other believers, so that I may share with them the gift You have given me. Help me not to wait to be moved by the Spirit, but to simply get moving! I thank You that our lives are not meant to be lived alone, but that You made us for relationships, both with You and with others. In Jesus' name, amen.

"Therefore, encourage one another and build one another up, just as you also are doing" (1 Thessalonians 5:11 NASB).

Day 28: In His Nail Pierced Hands

"But Thomas (called 'Twin'), one of the Twelve, was not with them when Jesus came. So the other disciples were telling him, 'We've seen the Lord!'"

"But he said to them, 'If I don't see the mark of the nails in his hands, put my finger into the mark of the nails, and put my hand into his side, I will never believe."

"A week later his disciples were indoors again, and Thomas was with them. Even though the doors were locked, Jesus came and stood among them and said, 'Peace be with you.'"

"Then he said to Thomas, 'Put your finger here and look at my hands. Reach out your hand and put it into my side. Don't be faithless, but believe."

"Thomas responded to him, 'My Lord and my God" (John 20:24-28 CSB)!

As you sit beside your loved one in a hospital bed asking God, "Why? Why my loved one? Why me, God?" God invites you to see the love He has for you! Touch the palpable love of God as Christ invites you to put your hand on His side where the soldier pierced Him with his spear (John 19:34 CSB). Touch the scars left by nails that were driven into His hands. See the place on His head where a crown of thorns was put on His head (Matthew 27:29 CSB). Look to the One who loves you more than His own life. Friend, in your sorrow, look to the One who made the ultimate sacrifice as He suffered in your place. In your sorrow look to the One who made a way for you to have peace with God (Romans 5:1).

"My sheep hear my voice, I know them, and they follow me. I give them eternal life, and they will never perish. No one will snatch them out of my hand. My Father, who has given them to me, is greater than all. No one is able to snatch them out of the Father's hand" (John 10:27-29 CSB).

Friend, when the world seems unrecognizable, recognize the voice of our Savior and have confidence in His outstretched hand. It was *His hand* that healed. "Jesus reached out his hand and touched the man. 'I am willing,' he said. 'Be clean!' Immediately he was cleansed of his leprosy" (Matthew 8:3 NIV). It was *His hand* that put the mud on the blind man's eyes as He told him to go and wash in the pool to be healed (John 9:6-7). It will be *His hands* around you when you go through that health scare when your marriage starts to fall apart, and when it feels like the very walls of your life are falling in around you. It is His hands that protect you when your world feels like it's being ripped apart with loss. It will be His hands that hold you up and you can entrust your sorrows and scars.

For all that He has done for us and suffered for us, trust in His goodness and faithfulness. As a child of God, there was nothing you did to earn God's love, so there's nothing you can possibly do to lose it. God does not choose His children for their beauty, talents, courage, or some specific character trait; as those gifts are all from Him in the first place! God loves us because He chooses to love us. Therefore, we can rest in the assurance, that His love for us is unconditional and we will never lose it!

Prayer

Heavenly Father,

It is Your hands that are holding up the universe, and it is Your hands that are holding up me. It was Your hands that endured the nails that would hang You on that cross for me. Thank You for the moment, on that hill You created, where You gave Your life for me. Help me to stand firm in Your promises and confidently trust in You. I rejoice in the life, peace, and joy I have discovered in Your precious hands. Thank You that as a child of God, my heart finds much delight in the safety and freedom of Your loving hands. Thank You that as Your child, Your hands will never let me go. I stand firmly in the hope I have in You. In Jesus' name, amen.

> "Fear not, for I am with you;
> Be not dismayed, for I *am* your God.
> I will strengthen you, Yes, I will help you,
> I will uphold you with My righteous right hand"
> (Isaiah 41:10 NKJV).

Day 29: My Weakness, His Strength

"Boasting is necessary, though it is not beneficial; but I will go on to visions and revelations of the Lord. I know a man in Christ, who fourteen years ago—whether in the body I do not know, or out of the body I do not know, God knows—such a man was caught up to the third heaven. And I know how such a man—whether in the body or apart from the body I do not know, God knows—was caught up into Paradise and heard inexpressible words, which a man is not permitted to speak. In behalf of such a man I will boast; but in my own behalf I will not boast, except regarding *my* weaknesses. For if I do wish to boast I will not be foolish, for I will be speaking the truth; but I will refrain *from this*, so that no one will credit me with more than he sees *in* me or hears from me."

"Because of the extraordinary *greatness* of the revelations, for this reason, to keep me from exalting myself, there was given to me a thorn in the flesh, a messenger of Satan to torment me—to keep me from exalting myself! Concerning this I pleaded with the Lord three times that it might leave me. And He has said to me, 'My grace is sufficient for you, for power is perfected in weakness.' Most gladly, therefore, I will rather boast about my weaknesses, so that the power of Christ may dwell in me. Therefore I delight in weaknesses, in insults, in distresses, in persecutions, in difficulties, in behalf of Christ; for when I am weak, then I am strong" (2 Corinthians 12:1-10 NASB).

As believers in Christ, we know that God doesn't look at physical traits and attributes, He cares about our character and our hearts! In contrast, we tend to place high value on attributes such as strength, power, and money; because that is what the world tells us to strive for every day. But God tells us something different. He cares about us. He pursues our hearts. Weaknesses, vulnerability, and helplessness are all characteristics that put us in the perfect posture to open our hearts and eyes to the beauty of the gospel, and our need for God. *It is when we are lacking that we see God in a new way.* "Instead, God has chosen what is foolish in the world to shame the wise, and God has chosen what is weak in the world to shame the strong" (1 Corinthians 1:27 CSB).

Whatever circumstances are causing you to suffer, know this, God can use it for good! Our initial reaction to suffering might be to plead with God to quickly, painlessly, and immediately remove it from our lives. However, that hardship may be the very thing that God uses to not only open your eyes to *see the light of the gospel but to reach others for Him.* Watch what God can do with your deepest hardship and circumstance! Be amazed by how God uses your weakness for your good, so that others may see His power at work in your life. *God can use your diagnosis, your divorce, your pain, your burden, your failure, and your brokenness because what you perceive as your greatest weakness may be your greatest strength.*

Friend, your greatest weakness may be the most powerful light illuminating the cross for others. *As you hold the hand of another in a similar situation, let your brightness radiate so that they may see the unshakeable hope you have in Christ.* When we begin to live out and share the gospel, our own hearts are awakened and filled with the joy of Christ. An inexhaustible joy is uncovered when we courageously and boldly live our lives wholeheartedly following Jesus. What if our hearts truly understood our desires should be focused on God's good and perfect will for us, trusting that in His sovereignty He knows what's best for us? Remember, that weakness in your life may be your greatest gift of all. Watch how God can use your vulnerability as a beautiful victory in Christ Jesus.

Prayer

Heavenly Father,
I joyfully bow before You, in praise and honor, for my mind cannot comprehend Your transcendence or sovereignty in all that You are doing. I desperately come to You on my knees, immersing my heart and mind in Your Word. I know that in You, and You alone, I find all I need. I draw near to You in my weakness, asking for Your strength to endure whatever circumstance I face. Lord, I don't always see You in the midst of my troubles, but I know You are working in the middle of my mess. Use my weakness for Your glory! I know and trust Your power is all I need and that You will give me what I need at the right time. I thank You that Your power is limitless and Your love is abounding. For I know, with all my heart, that You are all I need. In Jesus' name, amen.

"In the same way, the Spirit helps us in our weaknesses. We do not know what we ought to pray for, but the Spirit himself intercedes for us through wordless groans. And he who searches our hearts knows the mind of the Spirit, because the Spirit intercedes for God's people in accordance with the will of God" (Romans 8:26-27 NIV).

Day 30: Four Friends

"Seeing their faith, Jesus told the paralytic, 'Son, your sins are forgiven.'"

"But some of the scribes were sitting there, questioning in their hearts: 'Why does he speak like this? He's blaspheming! Who can forgive sins but God alone?'"

"Right away Jesus perceived in his spirit that they were thinking like this within themselves and said to them, 'Why are you thinking these things in your hearts? Which is easier: to say to the paralytic, 'Your sins are forgiven,' or to say 'Get up, take your mat, and walk'? But so that you may know that the Son of Man has authority on earth to forgive sins'—he told the paralytic—'I tell you: get up, take your mat, and go home.'"

"Immediately he got up, took the mat, and went out in front of everyone. As a result, they were all astounded and gave glory to God, saying, 'We have never seen anything like this" (Mark 2:5-12 CSB)!

The room was completely packed, wall to wall with people. The house was so full, that there wasn't even room outside the door, because they all came to see Jesus. Above Jesus' head, four men dug a hole through the roof and lowered a mat, carrying their paralytic friend, right down to Him (Mark 2:1-4). Jesus saw the faith that had driven these men to go to great lengths to get to Him. The paralyzed man came to Jesus for physical healing, yet Jesus knew what mattered even more was the spiritual condition of his heart. Jesus healed this man of his paralysis but first He forgave him of his sins. Our physical ailments are limited to this life, yet our souls exist for all of eternity.

How far are we willing to go in order to carry our friend's stretcher to Jesus? May the desire of our hearts mirror those who were willing to do whatever it would take to get others clear access to Jesus. Sharing the gospel is simply one broken and hurting heart telling another broken and hurting heart where they can find the Great Physician. How amazing that God chooses us, fragile clay jars (2 Corinthians 4:7 NLT), to receive the blessing of proclaiming the greatest news to the whole world! Spreading the gospel is the most loving and compassionate thing we could do for another human being, as we share with them the cure for the condition of our souls; that we are separated from God because of our sin. That the answer for our brokenness is only found in Jesus Christ! The One who loves you so much that He gave His very life for you. How good is His grace and steadfast love for us. In Christ, God offers us the free gift of eternal life.

What if you personally were gifted the most amazing gift of all time? What if you realized that this gift was not just for you, but for anyone who would also choose to receive it? Would you go and tell others about it? Of course, you would! You would joyfully run into the streets telling everyone that a life changing gift that promises eternal life is a gift to share. We should overflow with joy and passion to tell everyone that the Way to everlasting life is Jesus!

Prayer

Heavenly Father,
Thank You that You care not only about our physical bodies but for our souls as well. Just as passionate as these four men were to get their friend to Jesus that day, You are even more fervent in Your pursuit of us. You desire to restore us to Yourself that we might know the joy of knowing You. Teach my heart to be sensitive and kind to the hurts and sorrows of those around me; as I share Your message of hope. Illuminate my life so that I can be a bright beacon pointing to Jesus, the only One who can heal both body and soul. Shine a light so intensely in me, that it is impossible for anyone to see anything but You. Your Word says, "Those who are wise will shine like the brightness of the heavens, and those who lead many to righteousness, like the stars for ever and ever" (Daniel 12:3 NIV). Thank You that You have entrusted us to be Your witnesses and ambassadors, spreading seeds of the gospel throughout the world. Your love is for every nation and every individual. Help me to show them how precious they are in Your sight. In the name of Jesus, amen.

"We now have this light shining in our hearts, but we ourselves are like fragile clay jars containing this great treasure. This makes it clear that our great power is from God, not from ourselves. We are pressed on every side by troubles, but we are not crushed. We are perplexed, but not driven to despair. We are hunted down, but never abandoned by God. We get knocked down, but we are not destroyed" (2 Corinthians 4:7-9 NLT).

Day 31: I Am Fearless

Fear is the ultimate thief and enemy of our joy. Our constant companion in sorrow. It creates a home inside our hearts and invades our minds when we are most distraught, most alone, and most vulnerable. Fear robs us of a sunny day and blankets us in dread of tomorrow. Fear does its best to hold us confined within the prison bars of our hearts and minds, with bars as tangible as steel.

Friend, if you feel surrounded by the fear you have barricaded deep within your soul, you do not have to feel trapped a minute more. God welcomes us to cast all our anxieties on Him. *In Christ, we are no longer caught in the grasp of our fears, we are conquerors.* We can throw off the tendrils of worry and anxiety that entangles us and firmly stand in the strength of Jesus. Friend, do not allow Satan to gain even the slightest foothold, as arrows of fear fire against your armor of defense. When the waves of fear and life crash against the shore of your mind stand firm and know that, "When I am afraid, I will put my trust in You" (Psalm 56:3 NASB).

Allow Jesus to break free the chains of fear in your own life, those chains that have been holding you back from joyfully and confidently living God's plan and purpose in your life!

If there's life in your bones and breath in your lungs, live!

Press forward in the fearless boldness of Christ, asking for His strength when we lack the courage. Our God brings dead things back to life; there is nothing He cannot do. How does your fear fare in the light of the One who defeated death and the grave? God gives His children what we need, as He carries us through troubling times our hearts are discouraged and burdened. God's Word provides us with the sustenance and power we need. Christian, God has not given you a spirit of fear. You have been given power, love, and a sound mind (2 Timothy 1:7 NKJV). Don't stay *captive* to the fear and sin in your life but be *captivated* by Christ's love for you that was beautifully displayed on the cross.

The God who lovingly made you reminds you that He's had you yesterday, He's holding you today, and He's promised to take care of you tomorrow. Know who God is and all that He has done in your life. Jesus defeated the grave and you are no longer a prisoner to fear. Today is the day to trust Him with all your anxieties and lean into His promises. Say goodbye to scurrying, fretting, and worrying about the things of this world. Give your fears to Christ, and don't hold on to them a second more, as it is too much for you to carry alone. The question is not *if* fear will head your way, but *what will you do* when your fear stares you in the face and when discouragement starts to well up in your soul? The good news is that you already know what to do. "When I am afraid, I will put my trust in You" (Psalm 56:3 NASB).

Prayer

Heavenly Father,
You know how often I have allowed Satan to mix with lies in order to create scenarios that will cause fear in my life. I know

Your Word says, "For God has not given us a spirit of fear, but of power and of love and of a sound mind" (2 Timothy 1:7 NKJV). Help me to turn my struggles into praise! Cultivate a confidence in me that boldly rests knowing everything is in Your hands and I have nothing to fear.

Your Word says, "Be still, and know that I *am* God; I will be exalted among the nations, I will be exalted in the earth" (Psalm 46:10 NKJV)! Remind me that in every area of my life, You are working out all things for my good, that Your name may be glorified. Fill up my heart; overflowing with the Holy Spirit, empowering me today to live for You! As the Scriptures say, "I sought the LORD and He answered me, and rescued me from all my fears. They looked to Him and were radiant, And their faces will never be ashamed. This wretched man cried out, and the LORD heard *him* And saved him out of all his troubles. The angel of the LORD encamps around those who fear Him, And rescues them" (Psalm 34:4-7 NASB). I joyfully live today, knowing You are in control. I will not fear, for You are with me. The hope I have in You fills my heart and mind with delight. In Jesus' name, amen.

> "The LORD *is* my light and my salvation;
> Whom shall I fear?
> The LORD *is* the strength of my life;
> Of whom shall I be afraid"
> (Psalm 27:1 NKJV)?

Day 32: Wildflowers and Birds

Jesus said, "For this reason I say to you, do not be worried about your life, as to what you will eat or what you will drink; nor for your body, *as to* what you will put on. Is life not more than food, and the body more than clothing? Look at the birds of the sky, that they do not sow, nor reap, nor gather *crops* into barns, and *yet* your heavenly Father feeds them. Are you not much more important than they? And which of you by worrying can add a single day to his life's span? And why are you worried about clothing? Notice how the lilies of the field grow; they do not labor nor do they spin *thread for cloth*, yet I say to you that not even Solomon in all his glory clothed himself like one of these. But if God so clothes the grass of the field, which is *alive* today and tomorrow is thrown into the furnace, *will He* not much more *clothe* you? You of little faith!"

"Do not worry then, saying, 'What are we to eat?' or 'What are we to drink?' or 'What are we to wear for clothing?' For the Gentiles eagerly seek all these things; for your heavenly Father knows that you need all these things. But seek first His kingdom and His righteousness, and all these things will be provided to you. So do not worry about tomorrow; for tomorrow will worry about itself. Each day has enough trouble of its own" (Matthew 6:25-34 NASB).

Close your eyes and imagine you are walking through an

open field. Let your eyes soak in the magnificent beauty of God's creation. Feel the sun on your back, as it filters through the trees, sending glints of sunlight sparkling all around you. A meadow opens, revealing a field boasting of lilies, which are decorated from head to toe in vibrant color. Above you, hear the joyful melodies as a choir of birds happily welcome the day, without care or worry. *Friend, if God so lovingly cares for every detail in His creation and every creature that resides in it, will He not take even more care of You?* You were created in the image of God (Genesis 1:27) and He loves you more than you could possibly hope, ask for, or imagine. God doesn't automatically give us everything we want; He gives us everything we need. There is a key difference, and it's that God knows exactly what we need and provides it all at His perfect timing. "Keep your lives free from the love of money and be content with what you have, because God has said, 'Never will I leave you; never will I forsake you" (Hebrews 13:5 NIV).

"What is the price of five sparrows—two copper coins? Yet God does not forget a single one of them. And the very hairs on your head are all numbered. So don't be afraid; you are more valuable to God than a whole flock of sparrows" (Luke 12:6-7 NLT).

Find comfort in knowing that God knows every single strand of hair on your head. That's right! Every single one. Therefore, if God knows and cares about even the tiniest detail of your body, will He not continue to care for you in every circumstance and situation you face? God has lovingly provided your every need in the past, and because of that, you can trust Him to take care of you now and in the future. *Our Heavenly Father gives His children everything they need, therefore don't worry, child of God.* Your life has dignity, worth, and significant meaning. You are so dearly loved! May the sights and sounds of what Your eyes and ears drink in from creation, be a testimony of His love for You.

Prayer

Heavenly Father,
I rejoice, I sing, and I dance because You know everything about me! There is nothing Your eyes do not see. There is nothing that exists outside of Your power; therefore, I will not fear. You and You alone have everything in Your mighty hands. Your Word says, "For the eyes of the LORD roam throughout the earth, so that He may strongly support those whose heart is completely His" (2 Chronicles 16:9a NASB). Therefore, I will rejoice and be glad all the more. Strengthen me, Lord, strengthen my heart when I start to worry. I praise and thank You for the compassionate care You have for all You have created; how great is Your love! In Jesus' name, amen.

"How lovely is Your dwelling place, LORD of Armies. I long and yearn for the courts of the LORD; my heart and flesh cry out for the living God. Even a sparrow finds a home, and a swallow, a nest for herself where she places her young—near your altars, Lord of Armies, my King and my God" (Psalm 84:1-3 CSB).

Day 33: He Is My Refuge

"Whoever dwells in the shelter of the Most High will rest in the shadow of the Almighty. I will say of the LORD,
'He is my refuge and my fortress, my God, in whom I trust.'
Surely, he will save you from the fowler's snare
and from the deadly pestilence. He will cover you with his feathers, and under his wings you will find refuge; his faithfulness will be your shield and rampart" (Psalm 91:1-4 NIV).

Friend, the same question remains, *"Will you trust Him?"* Will you allow God to be your Fortress (Psalm 91:2), your Strength (Psalm 46:1), your Hiding Place (Psalm 32:7), your Deliverer (Psalm 18:2), and your Refuge (Psalm 46:1)? God is the only One who knows everything about you and invites you to take refuge in Him. He will never fail you! You may never know in this life why God allowed your pain, but we can thank Him for not leaving us to bear it alone. He sees when your heart, your spirit, is broken. When our souls become burdened by the troubles of life, the question is, "Will you allow Him to take care of you as He promises to do?" Are you ready and willing to take the leap from simply reading these words and hoping they are true—to wholeheartedly believing and trusting God at His Word? The Bible is unlike any other written word, "For the word of God *is* living and powerful, and sharper than any two-edged sword, piercing even to the division of soul and spirit, and of joints and marrow, and is a discerner of the thoughts and intents of the heart" (Hebrews 4:12 NKJV).

The Bible may be dry ink on a page that you can hold in your hands, but it is alive and active. We can trust His Word because His Word is Truth (John 17:17b). We abide with God in the difficult times and in the good times. He is our dwelling place. He is where our hearts find security, love, and a personal relationship with the Creator of the universe. If you feel shaken by your troubles and need Someone to hold you up in the midst of your struggles, He is right there, loving you. What joy we have when we delight in His Word. In the Word of God, we receive direction, nourishment, wisdom, and the way in which we should live our lives for God's honor and glory. So that, in the hard times, our hearts do not wither away or quake with fear, but we stand firmly planted in the promises of God.

In His Word, we discover God's nature and character. Our eyes and hearts are open to how we can trust God as we learn more and more about Him; about His faithfulness and goodness. To have a deeper relationship with God, we need to spend time talking to Him in prayer and studying His Word. The wonderful gift God has given us is that He has revealed who He is and what He has done for us in the Bible. We simply have to open it and read it! "But they delight in the law of the LORD, meditating on it day and night. They are like trees planted along the riverbank, bearing fruit each season. Their leaves never wither, and they prosper in all they do" (Psalm 1:2-3 NLT).

Prayer
Heavenly Father,
I'm closing my eyes and taking Your hand, trusting to go

wherever You lead me. I will follow You to the unknown places! For I believe, with all my heart, that the impossible is possible with You. When I am in an ocean of sorrow, Your love is deeper still. Your steadfast faithfulness is deeper than my doubts. Had You not taken me through my struggles, I would have never known the delight of Your mercies. Therefore, I will trust You all the more as I follow You. For You never leave my side. It is often in the unknown places, that the beauty of Your miracles shines brightest! Strengthen my wobbly legs and discouraged heart so that I can run forward with confidence and hope. My heart rejoices and overflows with the joy of knowing You are my strength, protector, and shield. In You, I have all that I need, and my soul is deeply satisfied. I patiently look to You for all I need and joyfully rest in Your will for me. In Jesus' name, amen.

"Because he has loved Me, I will save him;
I will set him securely on high, because he has known My name. He will call upon Me, and I will answer him;
I will be with him in trouble; I will rescue him and honor him. I will satisfy him with a long life,
And show him My salvation" (Psalm 91:14-16 NASB).

Day 34: Why, Lord?

"One day when Job's sons and daughters were feasting at the oldest brother's house, a messenger arrived at Job's home with this news: 'Your oxen were plowing, with the donkeys feeding beside them, when the Sabeans raided us. They stole all the animals and killed all the farmhands. I am the only one who escaped to tell you."

"While he was still speaking, another messenger arrived with this news: 'The fire of God has fallen from heaven and burned up your sheep and all the shepherds. I am the only one who escaped to tell you."

"While he was still speaking, a third messenger arrived with this news: 'Three bands of Chaldean raiders have stolen your camels and killed your servants. I am the only one who escaped to tell you."

"While he was still speaking, another messenger arrived with this news: 'Your sons and daughters were feasting in their oldest brother's home. Suddenly, a powerful wind swept in from the wilderness and hit the house on all sides. The house collapsed, and all your children are dead. I am the only one who escaped to tell you."

"Job stood up and tore his robe in grief. Then he shaved his head and fell to the ground to worship. He said, 'I came naked from my mother's womb, and I will be naked when I leave. The LORD gave me what I had, and the LORD has taken it away. Praise the name of the LORD!' In all of this, Job did not sin by blaming God" (Job 1:13-22 NLT).

Throughout the book of Job, Job suffers terribly. When Satan is allowed to strike him a second time, Job becomes covered, from head to toe with horrible boils (Job 2:7 NLT). After all his suffering and all he had lost, Job then endures further suffering through the words of his wife and of his friends. Job never received the reason for his suffering, but something miraculous happens, Job speaks with Almighty God Himself. In Job chapters 38-42, God spoke to Job in a whirlwind, wherein He asked Job questions. It is over the course of this questioning, that Job's eyes are opened to who God *truly* is. "Where were you when I laid the foundations of the earth? Tell me, if you know so much. Who determined its dimensions and stretched out the surveying line? What supports its foundations, and who laid its cornerstone as the morning stars sang together and all the angels shouted for joy" (Job 38:4-7 NLT)?

"Then Job replied to the LORD: 'I know that you can do anything, and no one can stop you. You asked, 'Who is this that questions my wisdom with such ignorance?' It is I—and I was talking about things I knew nothing about, things far too wonderful for me. You said, 'Listen and I will speak! I have some questions for you, and you must answer them.' I had only heard about you before, but now I have seen you with my own eyes. I take back everything I said, and I sit in dust and ashes to show my repentance" (Job 42:1-6 NLT).

In the end, Job's perspective of God changed and He saw God in a whole new way! God is in control, and everything is in His hands, including us. Our finite minds have nothing to fear in the hands of an infinite God. In this world, we know we will face troubles and that suffering is real. Our suffering opens our eyes to the brokenness deep within us and the brokenness of the world. Friend, how many times has this world let us down? We "think" it is God who has failed us, when in fact, we don't have the correct understanding of Him. We do not fully grasp His immense love, kindness, and faithfulness for us! As believers, we can go forward in faith and confidence knowing that we are, along with everything else in the universe, in His sovereign control.

Prayer

Heavenly Father,
I am sorry when I box You into a perspective that suits my own earthly needs and desires. Tear down the walls of my misconceptions, for You and Your ways are perfect. I kneel in awe at the mere thought of Your power, Your sovereignty, and Your wisdom. I trust everything into Your hands! In Jesus' name, amen.

"As the heavens are higher than the earth, so are my ways higher than your ways and my thoughts than your thoughts. As the rain and the snow come down from heaven, and do not return to it without watering the earth and making it bud and flourish, so that it yields seed for the sower and bread for the eater, so is my word that goes out from my mouth: It will not return to me empty, but will accomplish what I desire and achieve the purpose for which I sent it" (Isaiah 55:9-11 NIV).

Day 35: Home, A Place with No More Tears

Jesus said, "Do not let your hearts be troubled. You believe in God; believe also in me. My Father's house has many rooms; if that were not so, would I have told you that I am going there to prepare a place for you? And if I go and prepare a place for you, I will come back and take you to be with me that you also may be where I am. You know the way to the place where I am going" (John 14:1-4 NIV).

Beloved child of God, I want to tell you about our heavenly home. Heaven is a place of no more tears, no more death, no more pain, and no more curse of sin. Heaven is a future home where children of God will live forever with Him. One day we will go home and be reunited with our loved ones who also trusted in Jesus.

As believers in Christ, what peace we have knowing that heaven is not only a perfect place, but a perfect place where we will live with Christ forever. God promises that we will be with Him the moment we breathe our last breath. Our hearts rejoice in the homecoming that we, as believers, have to look forward to! We know that everything, good and bad, is but temporary in this life. The pain we suffered, the trials we faced, and the storms we endured; are all but for a short time compared to eternity. We have our hands and feet in this world, but we keep our eyes on heaven. *We joyfully and fully live the life God has given us, knowing that each and every day is a precious gift from Him.* Stand firm on God's promise, that as His children, we will one day be in the perfect presence of our Lord and Savior.

"For I consider that the sufferings of this present time are not worthy *to be* compared with the glory that is to be revealed to us. For the eagerly awaiting creation waits for the revealing of the sons *and daughters* of God. For the creation was subjected to futility, not willingly, but because of Him who subjected *it*, in hope that the creation itself also will be set free from its slavery to corruption into the freedom of the glory of the children of God. For we know that the whole creation groans and suffers the pains of childbirth together until now. And not only *that,* but also we ourselves, having the first fruits of the Spirit, even we ourselves groan within ourselves, waiting eagerly for *our* adoption as sons *and daughters*, the redemption of our body" (Romans 8:18-23 NASB).

As believers, we rejoice that there is more to come after our lifetime here on this earth. How extraordinarily heartbreaking it would be if life on earth was all we had. *What is the meaning of life if it all ends here with our time on earth, where injustice and pain for some runs concurrently with affluence and comfort for others?* Friend, this is where the glories of heaven fill our hearts with joy, as we know that life is not limited to this time on earth, but continues on with Christ, into eternity. It is the knowledge of this eternal gift that drives us to share the hope of Christ with those who do not personally know Him. This is why our hearts are joyfully and passionately brimming with boldness to share His message of hope and love, which is like a soothing balm to the hurting heart. We ask God to give us the joyful confidence to boldly proclaim the way of salvation. *That there is hope not just in this life, but a living hope in Jesus!*

"Blessed be the God and Father of our Lord Jesus Christ. Because of his great mercy he has given us new birth into a living hope through the resurrection of Jesus Christ from the dead and into an inheritance that is imperishable, undefiled, and unfading, kept in heaven for you. You are being guarded by God's power through faith for a salvation that is ready to be revealed in the last time. You rejoice in this, even though now for a short time, if necessary, you suffer grief in various trials so that the proven character of your faith—more valuable than gold which, though perishable, is refined by fire—may result in praise, glory, and honor at the revelation of Jesus Christ" (1 Peter 1:3-7 CSB).

Prayer

Heavenly Father,

As Your child, I rejoice! My heart overflows with joy, knowing Your children have their names written in heaven (Luke 10:20b). I praise You with all my heart, soul, and mind because of Your great mercy and love for us. You are so good! Lord, help me to live each and every day as a living testimony of Your grace. In Jesus' name, amen.

"Look, I am coming soon, and my reward is with me to repay each person according to his work. I am the Alpha and the Omega, the first and the last, the beginning and the end" (Revelation 22:12-13 CSB).

Day 36: The Fountain of Living Water

"The heavens are shocked at such a thing and shrink back in horror and dismay,' says the LORD. 'For my people have done two evil things: They have abandoned me—the fountain of living water. And they have dug for themselves cracked cisterns that can hold no water at all" (Jeremiah 2:12-13 NLT)!

Friend, what have you fashioned of your own design to replace the true and living God? Even the Israelites had turned away from God and chose to rely on false gods that were man made and imperfect. Where have you looked in order to fulfill the desires of your heart? *How easy it is for us to turn to our finances, our dreams, our spouses, our children, our passions, and things we own for our ultimate joy.* These things might not necessarily be bad in themselves but look how easily we rely on them to show who we are and what we strive for in our lives. How easily we forget God when we think we have everything we need.

Effortlessly, we turn away from Him when we feel self-sustained and self-empowered, as we sit in the driver's seat of our life. It is not until we face hardships and roadblocks that it feels like things are beyond our control. In our fear, we cling to our creaky and broken cisterns to help us, but then are perplexed and mystified that our broken cisterns are incapable of helping us in our time of need. We feel our world has been turned upside down when that very thing, idea, or person we have put all of our love and adoration into, fails us.

How quickly we turn to God and say, *"Where were You? How could this happen to me?"*

Yet God, in His gracious compassion, remains the same as He lovingly calls His wayward children back to Him. In times of pain, it can be surprisingly easy to simply numb the pain with empty remedies of the world to fill our brokenness and discontent. We look to empty, imperfect vessels to cope with the circumstances we face. These things might very well give us happiness for a short time, but everything, short of Jesus Himself, is ultimately unable to fill our heart's true longing and contentment. Only Jesus is the treasure your soul has been earnestly searching for in your life. How strange the hope we have in Christ must look to the rest of the world. It is an abounding hope that never fails!

"God, you are my God; I eagerly seek you.
I thirst for you; my body faints for you in a land that is dry, desolate, and without water. So I gaze on you in the sanctuary to see your strength and your glory. My lips will glorify you because your faithful love is better than life" (Psalm 63:1-3 CSB).

Prayer

Heavenly Father,
You alone as King, deserve full reign and rule over my life. You know of the things I have clung so tightly to, those things I have

given my foremost adoration, and put my identity and self-worth into. My grip on them was so tight that when they were pulled from my grasp, I fell to pieces. I felt lost. Yet, You never left me nor abandoned me, no matter how many times I have walked away from You. I rejoice that when I turn to You in faith and genuine repentance, You forgive me, for You are a forgiving Father. For I know repentance is a change of my mind and a change of my heart. The more aware I am of my inward brokenness, the more beautiful Your grace offered through Jesus becomes.

Show me how to seek Your ways and what is holy in Your sight. For I know that I cannot always trust my own heart to do the right thing. How often my own heart has led me to my darkest pain and deepest regret. But You see and know all things. Reveal to me anything I have left covered or hidden. Your Word says, "If I had cherished sin in my heart, the Lord would not have listened" (Psalm 66:18 NIV). I confess all my sins to You. Spirit of God, move in my heart! Take every room of my heart and make it Yours. In Jesus' name, amen.

"The LORD does not look at things people look at. People look at the outward appearance, but the LORD looks at the heart" (1 Samuel 16:7b NIV).

Day 37: Love Like Jesus

"If I could speak all the languages of earth and of angels, but didn't love others, I would only be a noisy gong or a clanging cymbal. If I had the gift of prophecy, and if I understood all of God's secret plans and possessed all knowledge, and if I had such faith that I could move mountains, but didn't love others, I would be nothing. If I gave everything I have to the poor and even sacrificed my body, I could boast about it; but if I didn't love others, I would have gained nothing."

"Love is patient and kind. Love is not jealous or boastful or proud or rude. It does not demand its own way. It is not irritable, and it keeps no record of being wronged. It does not rejoice about injustice but rejoices whenever the truth wins out. Love never gives up, never loses faith, is always hopeful, and endures through every circumstance. Prophecy and speaking in unknown languages and special knowledge will become useless. But love will last forever" (1 Corinthians 13:1-8 NLT)!

Friend, what would it look like for you, today, if you were to start loving those around you, as God loves us? How would your life change if you were to start freely loving others, without the expectation of receiving anything in return? As believers, we do not love out of obligation, we love out of the overflow of love Christ has for us. God cares about our hearts and is the driving force behind our motives. We love because of how Christ loves us. The love of Christ stands in sharp contrast against the backdrop of how the world loves. He loves us as we are and for who we are. He loves us when we are not "perfect" and when we break His commands. He loves us in our brokenness, sin, and shame.

"We love because he first loved us" (1 John 4:19 CSB).

When we realize His great love for us, we are then able to show great love to others because of the love we have been shown. When our soul is hurting, it can be incredibly easy to focus all our attention on our sorrow. Yet in Christ, we are healed and made new by His love for us, and our own desires are renewed and transformed because of that love. "But God demonstrates His own love toward us, in that while we were still sinners, Christ died for us" (Romans 5:8 NASB). What better illustration of God's love for us than the cross? God's love for us was put on full display as Jesus suffered and died so that we might have life in Him. What greater love is there? We joyfully accept and receive this gift God has for us. As Christians, we do not wait to be loved. We stand firmly and confidently planted in the love God has for us. As believers in Christ, we should be known for our love. "A new commandment I give you, that you love one another; as I have loved you, that you also love one another. By this all will know that you are My disciples, if you have love for one another" (John 13:34-35 NKJV).

What blissful wonders heal our hurting hearts as we serve those around us in loving mercy and compassion. What joy wells up as we reach out our hand to those in need. When we humbly step into the lives of others and hear their stories of struggles and hardships; watch the walls of pain and hatred begin to fall down. How quickly our perspective shifts when we see people through the eyes of Christ. When we act in love toward others, differences fade, and we begin to see how we are all broken and in need of love and kindness. At times when you are unsure of how to love, simply go to our Heavenly Father and ask Him how to love. We have a generous Heavenly Father who pours out His love and blessings. A Father in heaven who abundantly gives good gifts to His children, and lavishes His love on us each and every day. Today is the day to step out of your comfort zone! Embrace a new way of joyfully living that will begin to change your heart in ways you cannot imagine.

Prayer

Heavenly Father,

"I pray that from his glorious, unlimited resources he will empower you with inner strength through his Spirit. Then Christ will make his home in your hearts as you trust in him. Your roots will grow down into God's love and keep you strong. And may you have the power to understand, as all God's people should, how wide, how long, how high, and how deep his love is" (Ephesians 3:16-18 NLT). In Jesus' name, amen.

"Jesus said to him 'You shall love the LORD your God with all your heart, with all your soul, and with all your mind.' This is *the* first and great commandment. And *the* second *is* like it, 'You shall love your neighbor as yourself'" (Matthew 22:37-39 NKJV).

Day 38: God, I Will Praise You

"I will bless you every day;
I will praise your name forever and ever.
The LORD is great and is highly praised;
his greatness is unsearchable.
One generation will declare your works to the next and will proclaim your mighty acts. I will speak of your splendor and glorious majesty and your wondrous works.
They will proclaim the power of your awe-inspiring acts, and I will declare your greatness.
They will give a testimony of your great goodness and will joyfully sing of your righteousness.
The LORD is gracious and compassionate,
slow to anger and great in faithful love.
The LORD is good to everyone; his compassion rests on all he has made" (Psalm 145:2-9 CSB).

Today is a day for glorifying God and worshiping the One who created us! A day to joyfully worship our God, our Savior and King, with songs of praise, love, and adoration. Open your own Bible, carefully reading and reflecting on each and every word of Psalm 145, as your heart sings songs of thankfulness and praise to God. Raise your voice in gladness to the One who loves you, cares for you, and faithfully provides for you every day.

When our souls feel disheartened; the joy of worshiping God

allows our hearts to soar with gladness, for our hearts and minds are fixed on Jesus. Our worries, fears, and anxieties don't stand a chance when we focus all we have on making words of praise to our Creator and King. As we elevate our hands and voices to Him in worship, we experience a renewed sense of peace and joy that comes from Him. We were made to glorify God, not only with our words but with our very lives. We are to rejoice and be continually thankful, for we were made for His glory. What joy and satisfaction our souls find in our God.

Sing praises to God in the midst of your sorrow, when all you can do is barely mutter. Cry out to God words of praise and worship, for we discover freedom when we glorify God with our hearts. He is worthy of all our rejoicing and songs of praise. One day, every mouth and every knee will acknowledge that Jesus is Lord of all!

"For this reason God highly exalted him and gave him the name that is above every name, so that at the name of Jesus every knee will bow—in heaven and on earth and under the earth—and every tongue will confess that Jesus Christ is Lord, to the glory of God the Father" (Philippians 2:9-11 CSB).

Prayer

Heavenly Father,

I joyfully come before You with songs of praise as I throw off the worries and anxieties of the world and focus my heart on You! What joy it gives me when I lift up my hands in praise! You and You alone, I will worship all the days of my life. Thank You that worshiping You does something beautiful in my life. As I sing songs of praise to You, my heart is filled with thanksgiving as I recount all the blessings You pour down from above. I am reminded that You have always kept Your promises; and that in You my heart soars with hope. How can I ever praise You enough for all You have done? Therefore, I will worship You all the more. I thank You that You reach down for me in my brokenness and draw me to Yourself. You don't avoid my pain, but You meet me in it. I rejoice that the hands holding up the universe are holding me up. I rejoice in His nail pierced hands, as it is in them, I find life. I discovered a balm for my hurting soul. You are worthy of all the honor, praise, and worship; may I never forget Your mercies. I lift up my praise and worship to You for You never fail me. I rejoice because You lift me up and renew my strength when my soul is downcast. In the precious name of Jesus, amen.

"The Spirit of the LORD GOD is on me, because the LORD has anointed me to bring good news to the poor. He has sent me to heal the brokenhearted, to proclaim liberty to the captives and freedom to the prisoners; to proclaim the year of the LORD's favor, and the day of our God's vengeance; to comfort all who mourn, to provide for those who mourn in Zion; to give them a crown of beauty instead of ashes, festive oil instead of mourning, and splendid clothes instead of despair. And they will be called righteous trees, planted by the LORD to glorify him" (Isaiah 61:1-3 CSB).

Day 39: The Love of the Good Shepherd

"The LORD *is* my shepherd; I shall not want.
He makes me to lie down in green pastures;
He leads me beside the still waters. He restores my soul;
He leads me in the paths of righteousness for His name's sake.
Yea, though I walk through the valley of the shadow of death,
I will fear no evil; For You *are* with me;
Your rod and Your staff, they comfort me. You prepare a table before me in the presence of my enemies;
You anoint my head with oil; My cup runs over.
Surely goodness and mercy shall follow me All the days of my life; And I will dwell in the house of the LORD Forever"
(Psalm 23 NKJV).

Little Sheep opens her eyes to a new day. Her heart is filled with joy because she knows the Good Shepherd will be with her. As she gets ready, her thoughts quickly turn to all that lies ahead. Instead of allowing her mind to worry, Little Sheep goes into her bedroom and closes the door as she bows her head. As she pours out her day to the Good Shepherd, telling Him every detail of her heart, she finishes her time spent in the presence of the Good Shepherd thanking Him for every bit of blessings He has poured down from heaven that day. She praises the Good Shepherd that she is not in want, and thanks Him that He has already given her everything she needs. Little Sheep finishes her time in prayer by requesting that if there is just one thing she could do that day, it would be to give honor and glory to the Good Shepherd. Little Sheep then packs her tiny bag and heads to the local hospital, singing songs of praise to the Good Shepherd the whole way.

Inside the local hospital, Little Sheep takes her tiny bag and climbs the stairs to the third floor. Once there, she takes the time to greet the nurses, doctors, and hospital staff she meets along the way. She smiles at each and every one of them, as she takes a tiny flower from her tiny bag and gives them to each person she meets. She gives them a hug as she thanks them for all they do. Finally, she makes a left into the last room of the hall. Inside this room, is a Big Sheep, lying on a soft white bed. Little Sheep gives Big Sheep a kiss on his forehead as she takes a seat at his bedside. Little Sheep then spends the next few hours reading to Big Sheep from the Good Shepherd's Word (The Bible). Together, they laugh and cry as they reminisce over times the Good Shepherd had been beside them. As they remember how the Good Shepherd had been their Comfort, their Provider, and their Protector, their hearts fill with joy! Together, Big Sheep and Little Sheep sing songs of praise to the Good Shepherd, thanking Him for all the goodness and mercy He has shown them in their lives. After dinner, Big Sheep yawns as his eyes grow heavy with sleep. Little Sheep takes her cue and starts tucking-in the soft white covers to make Big Sheep feel nice and comfortable. Little Sheep says one last prayer and kisses Big Sheep on his head.

Little Sheep then makes her way back home, again singing praises to the Good Shepherd the whole way. As she gets ready for bed, she starts to yawn as her eyes grow heavy with sleep. She takes one last moment to go into her bedroom and spends time on her knees talking with the Good Shepherd. She thanks

Him for the gift of another day with Big Sheep, another opportunity to laugh and cry together. She thanks the Good Shepherd that even though Big Sheep is in a valley, they have nothing to fear. She praises the Good Shepherd that He is always with them, both when basking in the mountaintop sun or limping in the low of the dark valleys. She thanks the Good Shepherd that He always restores her soul and fills her cup to overflow. Little Sheep heads to bed with one last prayer, she asks that the Good Shepherd continue to watch over her and Big Sheep all the days of their lives. She falls asleep smiling, knowing that her prayer was already being answered.

Friend, you are loved by the Good Shepherd! God is the Good Shepherd who is always with His sheep, loving them, protecting them, and providing for their every need. His sons and daughters find their everlasting joy, peace, and contentment in the One who is always right there beside them. God personally knows each of His children, and they know Him. As we walk beside Him, trust Him, and follow where He leads us, we will see that His way brings the utmost peace and joy to our hearts. What a joyous life we discover, when we closely follow our faithful, righteous, and compassionate Savior and King. No matter what circumstance they face, He gives them the strength, protection, and comfort, they need every step of the way.

Prayer

Heavenly Father,
There is nowhere I would rather be, than following You, wherever You go. My heart delights that You have led me every step of the way, and I trust every step we take together in the future. Thank You that You never leave me alone or forget to give me what I need every day. You are all I need; You are my soul's delight. In Jesus' name, amen.

Day 40: Jesus Knows Your Sorrow

"He was despised and rejected by mankind, a man of suffering, and familiar with pain. Like one from whom people hide their faces he was despised, and we held him in low esteem. Surely he took up our pain and bore our suffering, yet we considered him punished by God, stricken by him, and afflicted. But he was pierced for our transgressions, he was crushed for our iniquities; the punishment that brought us peace was on him, and by his wounds we are healed" (Isaiah 53:3-5 NIV).

Friend, Jesus knows exactly how you feel. He knows your burdens, He knows your sorrow, and He knows what you have endured. *Whatever burden, heartache, loss, or brokenness you feel, He understands.* Jesus not only knows your sorrow and pain, but He also knows suffering itself because He Himself suffered and died on the cross, so that we may have life. Jesus personally stepped into our suffering, to save us. This is why when we look upon the wondrous cross, we are solemnly reminded of the overwhelming agony that Jesus chose to endure for us. Through faith in Christ, we may be healed, made new, and declared righteous in God's sight because Jesus' blood covers our sins.

"He himself bore our sins' in his body on the cross, so that we might die to sins and live for righteousness; 'by his wounds you have been healed" (1 Peter 2:24 NIV).

On the day that Jesus suffered on the cross for us, two criminals watched as the sinless Son of God painfully endured suffering at the hands of men. Both men deserved their crosses and the punishment they were receiving, y*et both had a decision to make about Jesus.* The criminal who chose to trust in Jesus knew and understood that he himself was a sinner. He simply repented and believed in Jesus, and Jesus responded that he would be with Him forever in Paradise (Luke 23:32-43). Jesus knew the faith of the criminal on the cross because He knew his heart. Each *of us has a decision to make about Jesus.* Just like the two men on either side of Jesus, we can either choose to reject Him or we can choose to surrender our life to Him. Friend, there is only one question that remains, "Have you personally received Jesus as Your Lord and Savior?"

What Jesus did on the cross for all of us was enough. We cannot do anything to earn our salvation and we rejoice that there is nothing we can do to lose it. We don't have to labor to be "good" to be made right with God, we receive the gift of salvation offered to us through faith in Jesus Christ. Both of those criminals had to decide about Jesus and so do you. If you are nodding in agreement and want to be a child of God, don't wait a second more! Simply cry out to Jesus. No exact words are needed. Simply talk to God from your heart. *Friend, repent and believe in Jesus.* Admit that you are a sinner in desperate need of a Savior and trust in Jesus. Look to Jesus for your salvation and be welcomed into the family of God!

"If you declare with your mouth, 'Jesus is Lord,' and believe in your heart that God raised him from the dead, you will be saved" (Romans 10:9 NIV).

Prayer

Heavenly Father,
Thank You that Jesus knows what it is like to be alone, tempted, misunderstood, and rejected. Jesus was mocked, shamed, abandoned, and suffered for me. As the Scriptures say, "For we do not have a high priest who cannot sympathize with our weaknesses, but One who has been tempted in all things just as *we are, yet* without sin" (Hebrews 4:15 NASB). Your Word also says, "For there is one God, *and* one mediator also between God and mankind, *the* man Christ Jesus," (1 Timothy 2:5 NASB). My heart cannot fathom what Jesus endured; as He was humiliated, tortured, and died for me. How can I not be moved by His sacrificial love? May I never lose sight of all Christ did for me! In Jesus' name, amen.

"Looking only at Jesus, the originator and perfecter of the faith, who for the joy set before Him endured the cross, despising the shame, and has sat down at the right hand of the throne of God. For consider Him who has endured such hostility by sinners against Himself, so that you will not grow weary and lose heart" (Hebrews 12:2-3 NASB).

Afterword

"These things I have spoken to you, that My joy may remain in you, and *that* your joy may be full. This is My commandment, that you love one another as I have loved you. Greater love has no one than this, than to lay down one's life for his friends. You are My friends if you do whatever I command you. No longer do I call you servants, for a servant does not know what his master is doing; but I have called you friends, for all things that I heard from My father I have made known to you. You did not choose Me, but I chose you and appointed you that you should go and bear fruit, and *that* your fruit should remain, that whatever you ask the Father in My name He may give you" (John 15:11-16 NKJV).

As a believer in Christ, Jesus calls us His *friend*. And just like any close friendship, the closer we are to Him, the more we get to know Him *personally*. We begin to truly trust Him. We get to know Him as our friend, and as Someone who is always there for us. Jesus is a Friend who listens to everything that we have on our hearts and our minds. Jesus is a Friend who made the ultimate sacrifice as He willingly laid His very life down for you and for me. Jesus is a Friend who not only cares about every area of our lives, but He cares about our hearts.

My greatest desire is that you would personally know Jesus as your Lord and Savior. You are known by Him, and you are loved by Him, but do you *know* Him? My hope is that in your sorrow you would begin to discover the love of God, a love that pulls you into His invitation of grace and hope through faith in Jesus. It was during a chapter of worry and fear in my own life that God opened my heart and eyes to who Jesus is and what He did on the cross for me. At that point, I had lived 23 years being active in a Christian church and school and yet had never truly heard the gospel in a way that I understood it. I *thought* because I went to church and did "religious things" that "of course" I was a child of God. I didn't understand that I had a choice to make. I didn't truly understand that God's invitation of salvation offered through Jesus was a gift that I had to personally receive. Jesus said, "Come to me, all you who are weary and burdened, and I will give you rest. Take my yoke upon you and learn from me, for I am gentle and humble in heart, and you will find rest for your souls. For my yoke is easy and my burden is light" (Matthew 11:28-30 NIV).

Jesus welcomes us to stop our toiling and striving in efforts to earn our way to God. Instead, He invites us to receive the gift of salvation offered through faith in Christ Jesus. Jesus already did everything that was necessary on the cross, and He continually offers us forgiveness for all of our sins. We simply need to repent of our sins and trust in Jesus. We come to Him as we are, for in Christ, we have *everything* we need.

It was at my breaking point that I came to the realization that, outside of Jesus, the stress and weight of life's burdens were too much to carry alone. *Jesus met me on my knees, in my time of need. In repentance and faith, I surrendered my heart and life to Jesus.* As I look back to that season of my life, I can see a beautiful picture of how God was working on my heart by strategically putting people and things in my life at just the right time. He used my husband, Bryan, to be a light and living testimony of how a person who loved Jesus lived out his faith. Right then, God sparked a new desire in me that had never been there, to truly know what was actually in the Bible. God used my worries to open my heart, and it has been Christ Himself who has carried me every day. I still wrestle against worry at times; however, I know where to go when my heart is troubled. I open God's Word and drink in His promises. His Word reminds my heart of Who He is and who I am in Christ. My worries don't stand a chance when exposed to the light of Christ!

Since that day on my knees, my life's desire has been to share the love, hope, joy, and peace I have discovered in Jesus. It is because of the sincere love I have for you that I write these words. Today, wherever you are, I reach through these pages to remind you of *God's abounding love for you.* The love of God is something that even now, I have trouble articulating into simple words. God is so much more than what our human minds can comprehend, and I take great joy in knowing that God is so much bigger than my understanding. For it is when life feels uncertain, that I find peace in the realization that I don't always have to know or understand everything.

I have discovered such joy in knowing that every piece of my life is in the sovereign and omnipotent hands of my Heavenly Father. I can rest assured knowing that God's way is perfect in all He does. No matter what I do or don't do, I know that I am loved by my Heavenly Father and that He cares for me. Even when I stumble and fall, He picks me up and gives me His strength and confidence to boldly go forward. I simply trust as I joyfully and abundantly live the life I have been given by God.

Friend, whether this is your first day knowing Jesus or you have been following Him for decades, my inspiration and encouragement to you is to joyfully live each day for Christ, whatever circumstances you are going through. Always remember that there is *meaning* to your life! If you have been desperately searching for satisfaction and meaning; there is only One place to find it within a relationship with God Himself. If you have been searching with a small light in the darkness for why you were placed in this life; with the family you have and the position you've been given, that reason is that you would know God and share that gift with others.

If we are honest with ourselves, there are moments in all of our lives when we have that overwhelming realization of our Creator. We are moved because we can see His glory in a very real and tangible way. We experience it in the grand moments of looking up at the moon and stars or standing gazing out over a mountain range. We experience it in the little moments of life, like a kind and compassionate hug from a loved one. Hold on to the moments that shout the love and glory of God in your life. Keep them front and center in your heart and mind so you can call on those memories when you feel down and discouraged. Use them as the catalyst to propel yourself out of your current situation and into the realization that the Creator of the universe loves you. He cares for you! He wants to hear from you. He desires to heal your brokenness, take away your burdens, and wipe away your tears in order to replace them with His peace.

Friend, the Christian message not only answers the questions related to our brokenness, troubles, and hardships but also gives us the reason why and how the world became fractured from the very beginning. When God made the world, it also was perfect in every way (Genesis 1:31). God gave Adam and Eve free will, the ability to choose right and wrong, to choose to love Him or disobey Him (Genesis 2:16-17). Unfortunately, they disobeyed God's only command when they took the fruit and ate it (Genesis 3:6). All creation was subjected to the curse because of sin (Romans 8:20). Sin fractured everything. We are separated from God because of our sins (Isaiah 59:1-2), yet out of His great love for us, God did not leave us in our broken state but put into action a rescue plan. From the very beginning, God lovingly pursued us and made a way for His wrath to be completely satisfied in Jesus' death and resurrection (Romans 5:8-9). "For the wages of sin is death, but the gift of God is eternal life in Christ Jesus our Lord" (Romans 6:23 NIV). Our sin debt against a perfect and just God was fully paid in Christ (Colossians 2:13-14). Therefore, when anyone accepts God's free gift of salvation through faith in Jesus, they are saved! "For it is by grace you have been saved, through faith—and this is not from yourselves, it is the gift of God—not by works, so that no one can boast" (Ephesians 2:8-9 NIV).

The troubles we endure in this life give us an overwhelming awareness of God, as the pain draws us closer to Him. If you have been reading these devotionals and have begun to feel even the smallest tug on your heart in the truth of what has been said, do not wait a second more to talk to God! Friend, simply cry out to Him. Come to God in prayer, with an open heart, and talk to Him as you would talk to a friend. You can come to Him at any time, any place, or wherever you are in the world. Perhaps you are even thinking that all this sounds so wonderful, but you have met a Christian or have been in a church where your experience was nothing like the goodness, love, and faithfulness of God you have begun to discover. On this side of heaven, brokenness and sin exists everywhere in this world. Therefore, instead of focusing on the brokenness, look to the One who was broken for us on the cross. Look to the One who never gives up on you, never turns His back on you, and who continues to invite you to know the only true peace of God through faith in Christ Jesus.

Friend, continue to remember that the love of God is the love of a Father, a perfect Father. In the story of the prodigal son, Jesus gives us an illustration of God's love for us. A father who looks into the distance and sees his wayward son making his journey back home. The father doesn't wait for him to arrive, no, he runs out to meet his son. The father kisses his child, as he throws his loving arms around him in a fatherly embrace (Luke 15:20). Friend, don't walk but run to your Heavenly Father. Run to your Heavenly Father, who throws His loving arms around us and welcomes us home no matter how far we have strayed or how long we have been gone.

"Anyone who listens to my teaching and follows it is wise, like a person who builds a house on solid rock. Though the rain comes in torrents and the floodwaters rise and the winds beat against that house, it won't collapse because it is built on bedrock. But anyone who hears my teaching and doesn't obey it is foolish, like a person who builds a house on sand. When the rains and floods come and the winds beat against that house, it will collapse with a mighty crash" (Matthew 7:24-27 NLT).

Printed in the USA
CPSIA information can be obtained
at www.ICGtesting.com
LVHW040820110824
787797LV00020B/36

9 781804 398241